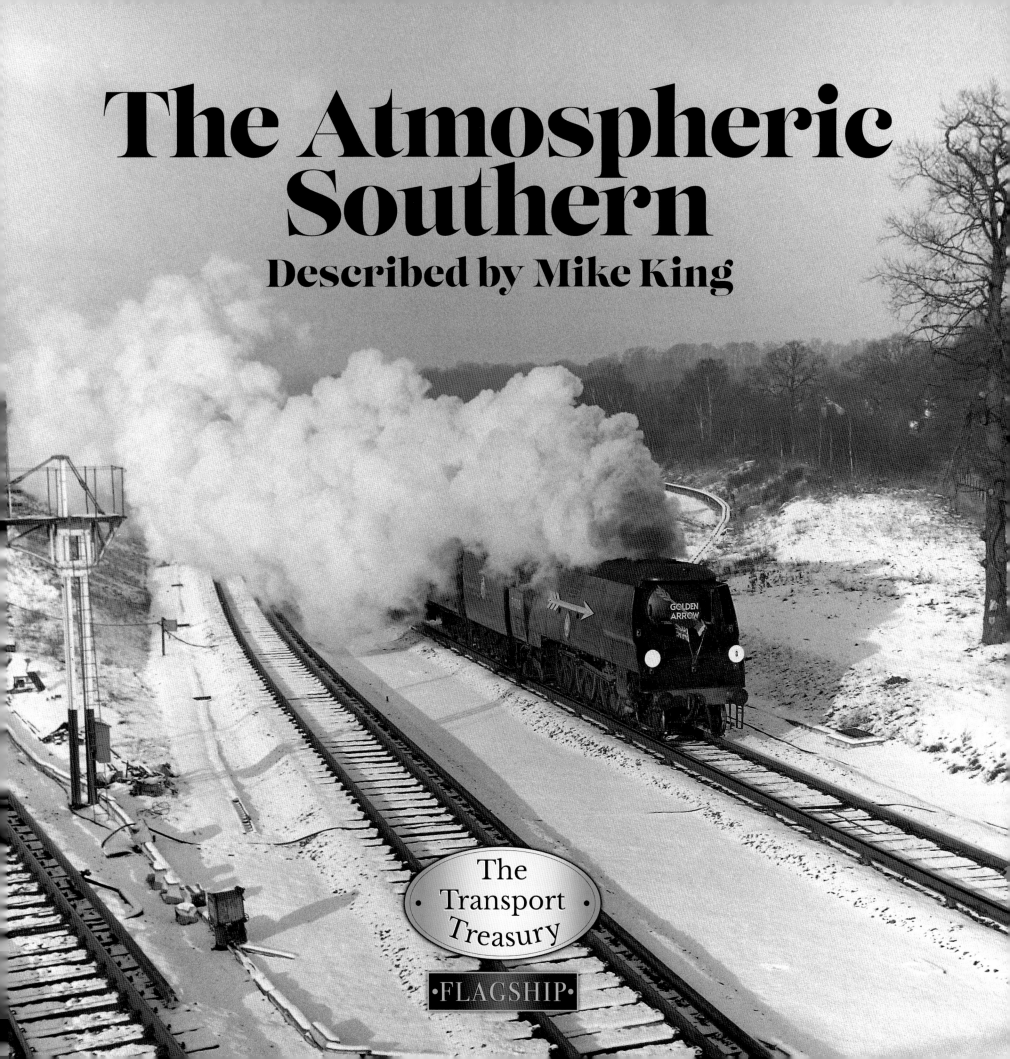

The Atmospheric Southern

Described by Mike King

The Transport Treasury

·FLAGSHIP·

Copyright: Images: Transport Treasury. Text: Mike King.

ISBN: 978-1-913251-52-9

First Published 2023 by Transport Treasury Publishing Ltd. 16 Highworth Close, High Wycombe HP13 7PJ

www.ttpublishing.co.uk

Printed in Tarxien, Malta by Gutenberg Press Ltd

Front Cover: An atmospheric scene at Tonbridge. West Country class pacific 34091 *Weymouth* comes through with boat train G3 up from the Ashford direction on 30 July 1960, watched by several enthusiasts. There is no doubt that the train has caught everybody's attention. No doubting the time either, so this would probably be the 2.50pm from Folkestone, due through Tonbridge at 3.43pm. Timekeeping of boat trains was always a little unpredictable due to weather conditions in the Channel, but there were always Q (conditional) timing paths to be used within the working timetables should the ferries be delayed, and this was one of them. The train includes the inevitable utility luggage van followed by at least ten rather mixed carriages; beginning with a Maunsell open second (ex-third) but the rest of the train could include SECR Continentals, Bulleids, BR Mk 1 vehicles and Pullman cars. After phase two of the Kent Coast electrification was completed, the loco moved to Salisbury and was withdrawn in September 1964; being one of very few locomotives to be cut up at Woods scrapyard, Queenborough, Kent in early 1965. An equally mixed train stands in the down through platform, with a Maunsell corridor second flanked by two BR Mk 1 vehicles: again, with onlookers. The author can remember steam on the Kent Coast; it was always worth watching and could be unpredictable in its variety! *D. Clark 1127*

Frontispiece: An evocative snowy scene at Petts Wood Junction. Original Bulleid Battle of Britain pacific 34085 *501 Squadron* negotiates the newly realigned down Chislehurst loop from Bickley Junction to Petts Wood Junction on 10 January 1960. The old alignment may be seen above the locomotive, and it will be noted that this was far more sharply curved and subject to a 30mph speed restriction. At this date the Golden Arrow left Victoria at 1pm (GMT) so the time will be after 1.30. This is confirmed by the shadows cast by the weak winter sun. Further signalling and permanent way works are continuing with staff on the track side in the left foreground. The solitary oak tree rather makes the composition. Other pictures at this location may be found later in the book. *D. Clark 1193*

Rear Cover: Sunlight and silhouettes. BR standards 80133 and 73037 stand outside the new shed at Nine Elms, sometime in early 1967. Because the connection to the main line at Loco Junction signal box faced west, locomotives invariably faced north while on shed, so that they would be facing down on leaving; ready to back into Waterloo or Nine Elms goods, depending on their next duty. So, most front-end photographs had to be taken into the sun at this location. Both these locomotives were late arrivals on the Southern Region. No 73037 was built at Derby in September 1953 and spent most of its life on the Western Region, coming to Eastleigh in March 1965. A move to Guildford took place soon after and then, finally, she moved to Nine Elms. No 80133 originated from Brighton in March 1956, spending time on the London, Tilbury, and Southend section before moving to the Western Region. She was transferred to Feltham in August 1964, with one more move to Nine Elms three months later. Both engines were condemned on 9 July 1967. *P. Hocquard 1264*

Introduction

In 2021, Transport Treasury published 'The Atmospheric Western'; a collection of the late George Heiron's Western Region photographs, while some years back Kevin Robertson (with Bruce Murray) featured the same gentleman's Southern pictures in their 'Waterloo to Ilfracombe' book (Noodle Books, 2009). It seemed logical, therefore, to produce something like 'The Atmospheric Southern' using Transport Treasury's extensive archive of Southern Region material.

So, what does the atmospheric Southern convey to most people? Hordes of bowler hatted commuters on their daily journey to the capital; day trippers off to the seaside; bucket and spade holidays in Kent, and on the Atlantic Coast Express to the West Country; Pullman trains like the Golden Arrow or Bournemouth Belle; hop-picker specials to Kent and Sussex; boat trains to Folkestone, Dover, and Southampton; the legend of King Arthur commemorated in locomotive names; bucolic branch lines with ancient tank engines hauling a pull-push set, perhaps? All these images I am sure, and many more, and a good many of them will be found between the covers of this book.

We will take a tour of the Southern Region; starting in London and making a clockwise journey around Kent and back into Surrey; then take an extended look at the railway crossroads that is Redhill; before travelling south and clockwise again around the central section to Tunbridge Wells, Brighton, Horsham, Midhurst, and on to South Western metals towards Eastleigh, Bournemouth and Swanage; west beyond Exeter before returning to the London area, Waterloo; and finally completing our journey at Nine Elms shed in 1967, weeks before the end of steam operation. I hope that you will enjoy the journey and the subjects seen along the way.

I have selected photographs from no less than thirteen photographers; some in profusion; others just one or two in each instance, but all are to be found amongst the Transport Treasury archives. A few details of these gentlemen (listed in alphabetical order) now follow; in many instances they will be well-known, but others much less so.

Dr. I. C. Allen – based in East Anglia, so many pictures taken in that area, however others were taken on the Southern, but only a few of these have come into the Transport Treasury collection.

A. E. Bennett – widely travelled, especially in London, the Home Counties, and the Isle of Wight.

David Clark – based in South-East London, so many photographs come from the railways of Kent.

Ken Coursey – again, South London based, and participated in many rail tours.

Leslie Freeman – first and foremost a South Western enthusiast, based in SW London; many of his pictures come from the western section of the Southern.

James Harrold – another widely travelled enthusiast, who put in over 50 years of photography.

Roy Hobbs – based at Reigate for much of his life and widely travelled but recorded the changing scene at Redhill over many years. Also, a bus enthusiast. Eventually retired to Hereford.

Paul Hocquard – had an eye for a good photograph; but admitted he took many less than satisfactory pictures to get the perfect composition. Those included here were all taken at Nine Elms in 1967. There are often half a dozen or more of each subject.

Nick Nicholson – South London based and worked for BR in 1950s and 1960s.

Henry Priestley – Headmaster of a school in Mansfield 1950-75. Also, a tramway enthusiast, whose collection came to the Transport Treasury via Colin Garrett. Lived to the ripe old age of 97.

R. C. (Dick) Riley – one of our most prolific photographers; favoured the GWR and the LBSCR. Was well-placed in South London to record the latter.

Neville Stead – widely photographed the industrial scene; minor railways and the BR "blue" era.

A. Swain – Alec was shed master at Willesden for some years; moving later to the Railway Inspectorate, so could tell a tale or two about accidents and near-misses; especially the latter!

The writer feels privileged to have known at least five of the above gentlemen.

Finally, I would like to thank Kevin Robertson and Andrew Royle from Transport Treasury with help in selecting the photographs, to David Gould for clarification of several points and brief biographical notes on several of the photographers, and to Roger Merry Price and his colleagues at the Bluebell Archive for help in identifying some of the workings depicted. They were beaten only once. But on that occasion, we all were!

Mike King, East Preston

We start our journey around the Southern on platform eight at Victoria, with the down Golden Arrow ready for departure at 2pm on 20 April 1957. Britannia pacific No 70004 *William Shakespeare* is all bulled up as befitting this prestige service; almost certainly the most important Southern Region train of the 1950s, and before the age of aircraft flights to the continent. Traditionally, the train would leave Victoria at 10.30 or 11am for a run to Dover, but from 5 October 1952 until 1960, the train was rescheduled to leave the capital at 2pm (1pm in winter) to run to Folkestone Harbour. The last stretch down to the harbour would be behind a SER R1 class tank loco, leaving the train engine to be turned and serviced at the small loco shed at Folkestone Junction. It would then take the empty stock tender-first to Dover Marine ready for a return from there around 6pm. From 1960 both journeys again ran via Dover and the morning Victoria departure time was reinstated. Two British Railways Britannia pacifics were allocated to Stewart's Lane shed from October 1952 and No 70004 was the usual engine; No 70014 *Iron Duke* would be used when the former was not available. In 1958, the two standards were transferred to the London Midland Region and Bulleid pacifics resumed the duty.

A few youthful (and not so youthful!) enthusiasts are watching while a line of luggage trolleys sits along the middle of the platform; presumably a little earlier these had carried passengers' luggage to the gangwayed bogie van at the front of the train. Note also the first passenger coach; not a Pullman, but a BR Mk 1 coach in crimson lake and cream. Travelling habits were starting to change and by 1957 the train regularly included a couple of ordinary coaches in the make-up. By its final run, on 30 September 1972, a minority of just three or four Pullman cars remained on the train and by that time they carried British Rail blue and grey corporate livery rather than the umber and cream of earlier years. Regrettably, it no longer seemed something special! *A. E. Bennett 2043*

Stewart's Lane depot served the needs of trains out of Victoria; both on the Central and the South Eastern sections; but it was not always so. Prior to 1933, the ex-LBSCR shed nearer the terminus at Battersea Park supplied the Central section motive power, but from then onwards all steam power requirements came from the ex-LCDR shed at Longhedge; rebuilt and renamed in 1934. This is a view across part of the yard by the coaling plant, which is on the far side of the LBSCR's South London line viaduct seen on the left of the picture. We are looking towards the enormous steel water tank that supplied the ten or more water columns situated around the depot. Visible are two ex-LBSCR E2 0-6-0 tanks, Nos 32103/5, ex-SECR P class tank No 31325, GWR 57xx pannier tank 8757, a mogul and the tender of a Bulleid pacific: whose identity will be revealed in the next picture. Some over-enthusiastic coaling appears to have taken place on 32105, while the P class is on coal stage pilot duty, moving the loco coal wagons under the coaler as necessary. The GWR interloper is from Old Oak Common and will have arrived with a cross-London freight or milk train via the West London line through Kensington Olympia. The date is 12 August 1956.
A. E. Bennett 1622

Top: And here is the Bulleid: a broadside view of West Country pacific 34091 *Weymouth*; at her home depot of Stewart's Lane on the same day having just been coaled up ready for another trip to the Kent Coast. This was the first of the final batch of light pacifics ordered after nationalisation, and the first to carry BR Brunswick green livery from new in September 1949. She was also the last member of the class to have an official naming ceremony. The loco was also equipped with hinged circular sandbox filler covers but these proved susceptible to damage and were soon replaced by the more usual sliding covers seen here. Unlike many of the Bulleids, this loco ran with the same 9ft wide tender throughout (No 3351) and was never ill-matched with a narrower tender as were many of the class. Regarded as a good performer while at Stewart's Lane, the loco was never considered as strong a performer when at Salisbury after 1961; indeed, the writer found the loco was a rare sight in London between 1961 and 1964. The conical concrete structure just seen on the left was the water softening plant. *A. E. Bennett 1621*

Bottom: Coming down to track level and turning through 90 degrees, we now look through the arches of the South London line viaduct towards the coaling plant at Stewart's Lane; but a little earlier, on 24 September 1955. Resident W class 2-6-4 tank No 31915 occupies the pit road that ends abruptly against the viaduct abutments: no buffers, nothing! The 15 members of the class were built between 1932 and 1936, primarily for cross-London freight traffic. This is where they spent most of their lives, only migrating further afield after 1960, when they could be found at Feltham: Eastleigh for the Fawley branch oil trains, and on banking work between Exeter St David's and Exeter Central. All were withdrawn from service between 1963 and 1964. Parts of the locomotives came from the ill-fated River tanks following the Sevenoaks derailment of August 1927 and for this reason were firmly banned from passenger service; despite a few attempts to use them as such over the years. On goods traffic they proved their worth, having good acceleration and braking power; essential when travelling over the busy suburban electric lines.
A. E. Bennett 932

The RCTS London River Rail Tour prepares to leave London Bridge station behind H class tank No 31518 on 29 March 1958. Beside it is 4-LAV electric unit 2926 on a semi-fast service to Brighton; duties they performed faultlessly for nearly 35 years. This was the unit involved in the South Croydon smash of 24 October 1947, which resulted in the destruction of the other motor brake coach No 10511 and its replacement by a 2-HAL motor coach. Departure time for the special was scheduled for 2.03pm, so we are within ten minutes of leaving. The tour ran to New Cross Gate, Deptford Wharf, Bricklayers Arms, Angerstein Wharf and thence to Blackheath, where ex-GER J68 tank No 68646 took over for the run along the East London line and into Liverpool Street, due at 5.24pm. The stock consisted of three ex-SECR pull-push coaches. Such Saturday afternoon rail tours were quite common in those days; many office staff worked a five-and-a-half-day week and so were free from lunchtime on Saturdays. Staff dress codes were often relaxed on the Saturday, with male workers being allowed to wear sports jackets and flannels instead of a suit, allowing them to go straight on to a football match, cricket, or rail tour! When the writer worked for Sir Robert McAlpine in the early 1970s there were still plenty of head office staff working there who remembered such arrangements. There were a few who participated in the rail tours as well!
L. R. Freeman 3294

A busy scene at London Bridge on 3 June 1960. We are looking across the three low-level ex-SECR platforms; numbers eight, nine and ten, with the six higher level lines (platforms one to seven, with the anomaly of one number missing; more recently corrected!) towards Charing Cross and Cannon Street behind. The ex-LBSCR station is out of sight to the left. At Platform ten on the left is 4-EPB unit S5163 on a train to Tattenham Corner via Forest Hill while another EPB unit is visible on the far right. In the centre we have Schools class 30917 *Ardingly* at platform nine heading the 4.40pm to Brighton via Oxted, Eridge and Lewes; a regular duty for this locomotive at the time. The head code displayed is wrong; the middle disc should be on the right of the smoke box but most signalmen along the route will not be fooled by this! At platform eight is BR standard 2-6-4 tank No 80094 which has just coupled up to the stock forming the 5.37pm to East Grinstead, which includes a SECR 10-compartment third (now second) to SR Diagram 52 as the front vehicle. By this date there were relatively few steam-hauled non-corridor coaches remaining in traffic. Behind that is a Maunsell restriction 1 low-window corridor second; another type fast disappearing from the Southern Region, followed by Bulleid 5-set 801 or 802. No 80094 is of interest in that it still carries a 6C (Birkenhead) shed plate but had been reallocated to Three Bridges in December 1959. The loco was built in October 1954 at Brighton Works and sent to Kentish Town shed. It was withdrawn in July 1966 from 70B Feltham and scrapped by Cohen's, Morriston in February 1967. Today the scene is totally different, and the station completely rebuilt to serve the needs of the 21st Century.
D. Clark 0906

The approach to London Bridge, showing the multiplicity of tracks coming in from Kent and Sussex. The photographer is travelling in what looks like a 4-SUB unit on a Central Section service into the terminal part of the station while an EPB unit runs down showing head code 10 – Charing Cross to Bromley North via Parks Bridge Junction – but the main subject of the two photographers' attention (we can see another man with camera in hand in the leading coach) is LNER J50 tank No 68926 on a goods train to, probably, Hornsey yard, timed at 6.47pm on 20 August 1960. This will take the sharply curved and steeply graded spur round towards Blackfriars and Holborn Viaduct beyond London Bridge, and then dive down Snow Hill incline to the Metropolitan widened lines to Farringdon; taking the Hotel Curve under Kings Cross station to emerge alongside platform 16 (later renumbered 14 and now long gone) and then enter Gasworks Tunnel to reach its destination. Not a route for engine men with asthmatic problems; this was a notoriously smoky and sulphurous journey and often one where delays could be encountered. Indeed, there was a general embargo on cross-London freight traffic during the rush hours, so this could be the first goods train through London Bridge since about 4pm. Had there been a Jinty on the front then the train would take a slightly different route to just north of St. Pancras and the Midland lines to Kentish Town and Cricklewood. The train is all van-fits, most of which are standard BR ventilated vans, but a BR pallet van with offset doors is nearest the cameraman. These were an unmitigated disaster as they were often loaded unevenly due to the position of the doors and once whisked up to speed behind a diesel locomotive, they were prone to derailment. As a result, all 2388 vans built were removed from service by the mid-1960s; many being sold or found alternative uses as departmental and static stores vans; places where they could cause no harm! Several have been acquired by preservation societies; often having been purchased from the Port of London Authority's railway system who acquired quite a few of them. In the background the dome of St. Paul's Cathedral can be seen, and the jibs of cranes in the Pool of London. Today's skyline looks very different indeed! *D. Clark 0703*

Alongside platform 16 at London Bridge, at some point between 1959 and 1961, U1 class No 31907 is ready to leave with a train for Tunbridge Wells West via Oxted and Hever; the driver looking back for the right-away. The locomotive still carries a 73A Stewart's Lane shed plate, but duty 296 falls in the series allocated to Tonbridge. The loco was re-allocated to Tonbridge in mid-1959, so this is the suggested date for the picture. However, identification of the train has baffled all the experts. Tonbridge duty 296 was for a train from Victoria to the Oxted line; not from London Bridge, so unless engineering works have caused a diversion and without an exact date, we are guessing. At this date there was a 4.20pm steam departure from platform 16 at London Bridge, but this was to Tunbridge Wells West via East Grinstead rather than via Hever, so if it is this service, both the engine head code and duty number are wrong! As a class, the U1s seem to have been less than popular and were regularly re-allocated from shed to shed during their working lives; leading to the conclusion that staff wanted rid of them. On the left, a 4-LAV electric unit waits to leave on a semi-fast service to Brighton and passengers are just making their way along the platform to join the train. Note the shunting bell plunger mounted on the signal post, but the significance of the half and full sign is not known – or has it just been put there as somewhere convenient to leave it? *R. Hobbs 1335*

M7 class 0-4-4 tank 30050 has charge of an enthusiasts' special at Deptford Wharf on 31 May 1959. This was The Thamesider Special organised by the Southern Counties Touring Society and made a circular tour starting from Clapham Junction encompassing Willesden Junction, Richmond, the Kingston loop, Putney, Brixton, Nunhead, Angerstein Wharf, Bricklayers Arms and Deptford Wharf, before returning to Clapham Junction via Streatham Hill and Balham. The stock was an ex-LBSCR pull-push set. If on time, the train was at Deptford for just ten minutes; between 6.40 and 6.50pm; and the participants are clearly getting out and about recording the scene with their cameras. The location was served by a branch off the LBSCR at New Cross Gate and the River Thames wharf is behind the photographer, and across Grove Street level crossing. This was by no means the only rail tour to visit the location during the late 1950s and repeated some of the locations visited by the London River Rail Tour of March 1958. In earlier years, traffic was mostly coal and timber, but by the late 1950s, it was more general in nature. Although a Southern Region depot, only two ex-Southern wagons may be seen; the two semi-elliptical roofed vans right of centre. Closure came in 1964 and the area today is unrecognisable and almost entirely given over to housing development. *A. E. Bennett 4848*

D1 class 4-4-0 No 31489 arrives at a busy Woolwich Arsenal station with the 10.14am Deptford-Ramsgate excursion on Whit Monday 18 May 1959: the fact that a reporting number is carried confirms a day excursion to the Kent Coast. Indeed, the photographer himself journeyed onwards to Faversham, as we shall see later. The train would have started from Rotherhithe Road carriage sidings, and Deptford would have been the first advertised pick-up. This was not the first station to serve Woolwich; the first was Woolwich Dockyard which opened with the line in July 1849. A more convenient station located to the east for the town centre followed in the next November and was reconstructed into the form seen here during 1906. Electrification reached here and to Dartford in 1926, extending to Gravesend just four years later, and to Gillingham in 1939. Steam would have become a rare sight here just a month after the picture was taken with the switch-on of phase one of the Kent Coast electrification to Ramsgate and Dover via North Kent. Reconstruction of the booking hall at street level took place in 1996 in a style reminiscent of Ashford International, and further changes took place in 2009 with the arrival of the Docklands Light Railway. *A. E. Bennett 4764*

The 10.30am Victoria to Dover Marine boat train (due there at 12.17pm and the relief to the Golden Arrow, which followed) comes through Bromley South at 10.52am on 4 September 1960 behind the last Southern Railway built light pacific; No 34070 *Manston*: one of six members of the class to be named after airfields involved with the Battle of Britain. It was also the last to lose malachite green livery in March 1953. The writer used to see this train come through Folkestone Junction during 1960 and recalls it was often headed by No 34092 *City of Wells*. The head code indicates that the train will take the spur round from Bickley Junction to Petts Wood Junction and Orpington to run down the SER main line through Tonbridge and Ashford; known to the writer as boat train route number one. There were at least four possible boat train routes to Dover; the others being via Otford, and either back to the main line at Sevenoaks, or via Maidstone East or through North Kent via Chatham. The stock is remarkably uniform for a boat; with just Bulleids and BR Mk1 coaches visible although there might be a Pullman to provide catering services further back. This was normal on the Central and South Eastern sections, where the Pullman Car Company had historically been contracted to provide all catering facilities. Things were different on the South Western section, where railway-owned catering staff and cars were also employed. The local goods yard is still busy with domestic coal traffic, but maybe not for much longer. *D. Clark 0746*

The Chislehurst Loops

Prior to the formation of the South Eastern & Chatham Railway in 1899, the two Kent railway companies operated almost independently: often in direct competition. Their main lines crossed one another east of Bickley or south of Chislehurst; depending on where your company allegiance lay! The new company was a working union, rather than a take-over by one or the other. Its' first task was to connect both sets of lines, and to this end contractor Price and Reeves were appointed to construct four interconnecting spurs which would allow maximum flexibility of service; enabling trains from the Kent coast to London to run to either the former SER or the LCDR termini. Ultimately, this allowed all continental boat services to be concentrated on Victoria, whereas previously ex-SER boat trains had run to Charing Cross instead. The four spurs were quite long, and it took until September 1902 for the first ones to be opened: two years before completion in June 1904. In 1958, work began to realign them to increase running speeds through the junctions as part of the Kent Coast electrification improvements, and in more recent years further layout changes have taken place.

Battle of Britain loco No 34071 *601 Squadron* negotiates the newly aligned down loop from Bickley Junction towards Petts Wood Junction on 28 February 1959 with the down Golden Arrow. The disconnected old loop may be seen curving round behind the locomotive and the new formation is considerably straighter allowing line speeds to be increased from 30 to 50mph and is better connected with the lines coming from Bickley. Note also that there will be a direct connection to both down lines towards Petts Wood without having to negotiate a crossover; this track has yet to be ballasted so almost certainly has not yet been brought into use. The signalling is also being revised as there is a missing doll on the bracket coming down from Chislehurst; the crossover to which it refers has been replaced by the yet unused one in the left foreground. No 34071 does not look quite as pristine as Stewart's Lane might like, and as she is a Dover engine, possibly a substitution at the last minute. This was the first true Battle of Britain loco: 9ft wide over cab and tender with a water capacity of 5500 gallons, whereas Nos 21C149-70 remained 8ft 6in wide and were almost identical to the earlier West Countries. The train on this occasion is all-Pullman; just seven cars including Pegasus containing the Trianon Bar in the centre, with a luggage van topping and tailing the formation. A light Winter Saturday load perhaps? *D. Clark 0004*

Top: The same location but a few months later, 7 June 1959. The old connecting spur has been removed completely, and the new connections ballasted, and it is now the turn of the weed killing train to spray the new formation. N class mogul No 31410 (the one with small upward extensions to the smoke deflectors) oversees the train which is probably propelling over the junction; the fireman is keeping a close lookout. No, it isn't the driver: the last eight moguls (1407-14) had left-hand drive! The brake van is DS455; one of the fifty Diagram 1581 15-ton pillboxes built in 1934 for lighter duties. At the other end of the train will be two utility van conversions; mess van DS470 and spray van DS471 and in between, up to six tanks converted from old locomotive tenders; one of which may just be seen. There was one other weed killing train of similar formation, but this had cylindrical tanks mounted on old tender underframes. Note that all semaphore signal arms have been removed and the junctions are now controlled by colour lights. *D. Clark 0144*

Bottom: Another week on, and the Arrer negotiates the new junctions behind BB 34085 *501 Squadron*; a regular performer around this time and certainly bulled up to perfection on this occasion; 14 June 1959. The train is now formed of a BR Mk1 full brake in crimson lake and cream, followed by a Bulleid corridor first in green, another Mk 1 in crimson lake and cream, then the Pullman cars. The track below left does not look like it is in regular use. A similar view but taken in snowy conditions may be found on the title page. *D. Clark 0195*

On 29 March 1959, but in the other direction; N class mogul 31406 negotiates the up spur from the Chatham line (just visible in the background) round towards Chislehurst station with a freight from Dover or Ashford to Bricklayers Arms via Maidstone East, including empty conflat D's and SNCF ferry wagons. This mogul is right-hand drive; note the reversing rod visible on this side and compare it with 31410 in the earlier view. This spur required far less work to achieve faster speeds, so at this point does not look very different from before; perhaps just new flat-bottomed rails in place of the earlier bull-head pattern. The connections at each end required some realignment. The platelayers hut looks positively antediluvian! *D. Clark 0012*

Crompton D6508 hauling 11 coaches up near Petts Wood, timed at 10.07 on 18 June 1960. Head code 4 indicates Ramsgate or Margate to Charing Cross via Dover, Folkestone, and Tonbridge, so this is likely to be the 7.26 from Margate, on time too, so an early outing for the diesel on a main line service. The train reporting number is 209, and there is a chalked departure time on the top of the board, but it cannot quite be read. These locomotives are better known nowadays as class 33 but to us spotters of the day they were just "D six-fivers". They were externally almost identical to the Birmingham RCW Co D5300 class already to be found on the London Midland Region; but by removing the steam heating boilers from the design, the Southern achieved type three power rating instead of type two for the LM class; more space was available for the power source. However, as most SR stock was then only steam-heated, they could only be used on passenger haulage during the summer months. As more stock was dual or electrically-heated the problem disappeared, but back in 1960 this issue was addressed by the temporary transfer of up to twenty Sulzer type two locomotives, as noted in a later caption. D6508/33008 eventually went through the usual livery changes for the class, but in March 1992 was returned to green livery as D6508, named *Eastleigh*, and has subsequently been preserved. The train comprises Maunsell restriction 4 three-set 194 or 195, a loose Maunsell flush-sided third (now second) of 1935 with a BR Mk 1 seven-set including a Maunsell buffet car on the rear; the train was diagrammed just for one of sets 278 or 280. The other coaches appear to be "extras". *D. Clark 0963*

Observations at Orpington

This group of pictures were all taken just north of Orpington station during 1959 and 1960. Orpington was for many years the terminus of the Southern's inner suburban electrification of 1925, and the end of the four-track layout. Beyond here, the line becomes double track and, although outer suburban electrification to Sevenoaks took place in 1935, the line southwards changes somewhat in character. The station was rebuilt and much enlarged by the South Eastern in 1904, providing four through platforms and two London-facing bays, with extensive carriage sidings and a locomotive shed to provide power for the numerous steam-hauled suburban trains. The latter was replaced by more storage sidings in the 1925 electrification, since when the large carriage shed just north of the station was built. In more recent times, this shed has been removed and further rebuilding of the station has taken place. The track layout has been rationalised but there are now two more passenger platforms, bringing the total to eight.

The 12.18pm Hither Green to Tonbridge yard freight approaches Orpington on the down local line in June 1960 behind N class mogul No 31829, passing the 1925 carriage shed. It was reputed to be the largest on the Southern Railway with a length of 1050 feet and capable of holding no less than 128 coaches. The train has a fitted head of ten vans; most of these being modern BR vehicles but at least one each of LMS, LNER and Southern origin are visible. Beyond that are unfitted opens, minerals and a few more vans, with the obligatory brake van on the rear; about 40 wagons in total. The train has a clear run through the station and onwards towards Chelsfield, as indicated by the distant signal at off; so, getting a good run at the rising grades towards the summit at Knockholt. Also note that despite two rounds of electrification, the signalling remains semaphore throughout. This was often a feature of Sir Herbert Walker's electrification planning; all done with the minimum of capital expenditure. A 4-EPB unit stands in the up side headshunt. *D. Clark 1004*

In the opposite direction, at 5.30pm on 4 June 1960, another N class mogul; No 31824, calls at Orpington to drop off a STEF continental refrigerator van into the goods yard behind the photographer. Whether this was a scheduled call, or enforced to drop off a defective vehicle, is not known. The train, thought to be the 3.20pm Dover Marine to Hither Green yard, was scheduled to pass Orpington at 5.23pm. The picture is taken from footbridge No 166, which spans six tracks at this point and pierces the roof of the carriage shed, so walkers would pass between the two facing asbestos gable ends of the building. The goods yard included a goods transhipment shed, cattle dock (almost certainly long disused by this time) and coal pens among the eight sidings, and by the 1960s several were conductor-rail equipped for berthing even more suburban stock. Notice the elevated miniature shunt signal to the left of the locomotive; this would have a yellow arm with a black vertical stripe meaning that drivers could pass it at danger if moving along the headshunt but would have to obey the aspect when moving over the crossing and onto the up main line. In the background we can see footbridge No 165, a little further north. We shall move towards that location for the next pictures. *D. Clark 0932*

A rather sunnier day on 5 July 1959 and a very different locomotive, on a similar duty as in the previous picture, but viewed from bridge No 165. Sulzer type two diesel No D5002 is about to pass the up advanced starter signal (the relay boxes for this are visible to the left) with a van train from Dover to Bricklayers Arms. First in the formation is a Blue Spot fish van in its smart white livery, followed by the usual selection of SR utility vans. The Southern had ordered a batch of new type three diesels from BRCW in December 1957; those that became better known to us enthusiasts as Crompton's or type 33 locomotives, but it was soon apparent that delivery of these would not take place until 1960; some time after phase one of the Kent Coast electrification. As a stopgap, twenty Sulzer locomotives (D5000-19 and later to become class 24 diesels) were intended to be diverted from the London Midland Region and these began to arrive at Hither Green shed in early 1959. However, it was soon discovered that these were heavier than anticipated and could not be used on all the duties envisaged for them. Perhaps for this reason that not all twenty arrived and some of those that did had their train heating boilers removed to reduce their axle weight; rather reducing their usefulness as those so modified could not be used on passenger trains during periods of cold weather. The writer noted all except D5015/19 in Kent during this period, so maybe these two never arrived. The rest remained on South Eastern section services until finally returned to Willesden by July 1962; sometimes piloting the new class 33 diesels simply to provide train heating facilities. *D. Clark 0257*

A matching of standards. Taken just south of the previous picture, again on 5 July 1959; where a footpath runs alongside the line; note the photographer's bicycle on the right, sees BR class 5 4-6-0s 73086 and 73087 pass each other just north of the carriage shed at Orpington. No 73086 is on a down Kent Coast working while 73087 is hauling an inter-regional train of LMS stock towards Kensington Olympia and the north. Ten of these locomotives went new to Stewart's Lane depot in 1955, with ten more to Nine Elms soon after. From late 1959, they were bestowed with names formerly carried by Urie King Arthur locomotives; No 73086 becoming *The Green Knight* and No 73087 *Linette*; both being characters from the King Arthur legends. Once full electrification of the Kent Coast lines was completed in 1961, all migrated to the South Western section where some saw out the end of steam working in July 1967. *D. Clark 0423*

Going down the ex-South Eastern's main line towards Tonbridge, the summit of the climb through the North Downs is reached at Knockholt, where rebuilt Bulleid pacific 34100 *Appledore* breasts the summit with the down Golden Arrow on 31 March 1961. Steam haulage of the train had less than three months to go and Appledore would oversee the final steam working on 11 June; watched and photographed by many along the route. Indeed, the loco had been on the duty constantly in that period; with BB rebuild 34088 being the other regular engine. On this day, there do not appear to be ordinary coaches in the train, but the luggage van on the front is a green painted BR general utility van. Non-railway observers in Kent might conclude that the locomotive was named after the village on the edge of Romney Marsh rather than the West Country town beside the River Torridge; the small scroll stating West Country Class below the nameplate being difficult to read as the loco flashed past at 60mph! After her Stewart's Lane days were over, the engine moved to Brighton and thence to Salisbury in September 1963. The writer did not see the engine through Surbiton (his most regular spotting location) again until that time and his last sighting was at Basingstoke shed in June 1967, a fortnight before withdrawal. *D. Clark 1993*

D1 class 4-4-0 No 31739 comes up past the timber clad Polhill signal box with empty stock comprising just two coaches of former Hastings line restriction 0 three-set 214 and a 'BY' four-wheeled passenger brake van on 1st July 1960, timed at 10.45am. This working took some time to trace but arrived at Tonbridge as the 9.30am from Ashford and then ran empty from Tonbridge to Rotherhithe Road sidings. The same train formation is seen in a later picture at Paddock Wood, albeit then with a Schools class locomotive in charge. The train arrived at Tonbridge at 10.22am and then left empty four minutes later. By this time, the Hastings line steam stock was all but redundant as the service was in the hands of the new diesel-electric units and the vehicles began to turn up in other locations, even west of Exeter on occasion. A few restriction zero coaches were retained until 1962 for use on overnight newspaper trains to Hastings and this is how the stock seen here began its day; on the 5.45am London Bridge-Hastings service, travelling to Ashford at 8.34am. As may be seen, Polhill box was very much in the countryside and Polhill Tunnel is behind the photographer, while Dunton Green is away to the south. However, the location today is less peaceful with the M25 traffic roaring past just to the west. New conductor rails are lying in the four-foot in preparation for upgrading in time for phase two of the Kent Coast electrification which went live on 12 June 1961. Also visible behind the train is a precast concrete permanent way hut of a type seen all over the Southern and manufactured at Exmouth Junction concrete works as well as rail-built signals controlling both directions. The down signal is mounted on the right-hand side of the line to make it visible to trains on the long curve beyond Polhill Tunnel and has a co-acting arm at high level; visible above bridge 182: known as Twittons; upon which the photographer is standing. Of course, the signal box is no more; all that may be seen today is a radio mast and featureless switch room on the other side of the bridge. Communication methods have changed! *D. Clark 1015*

Top: North of Dunton Green, we see brand new Crompton D6506 heading an up train of ferry vans over an imposing brick arch bridge spanning The Pilgrims Way; bridge No 184; otherwise just a minor country lane. The run may be a test, as there are staff visible in the rear cab of the locomotive and the date is recorded as 7 May 1960 at 5.13pm and may possibly be the same working as seen at Orpington in a previous picture; the 3.20pm Dover Marine-Hither Green yard. As is well known, the Cromptons were one of the most successful of the new breed of British Railways diesel locomotives and proved to be very capable machines; a few of which lasted in BR service until 2001. No less than 29 of the 98 examples are in preservation; indeed, most heritage railways seem to have one, and several are still passed to run on the national network today. D6506 was badly damaged in a freight train collision at Paddock Wood on 8 December 1961 but was subsequently repaired and lasted until August 1991. The only member of the class destined to have a very short life was D6502, broken up after a serious freight train collision at Itchingfield Junction, south of Horsham, on 5 March 1964. It was so badly damaged that it was cut up on site; indeed, the writer came past the tarpaulin covered locomotive on its side soon afterwards, and it was very evident why both the loco men perished. *D. Clark 1330*

Opposite Bottom: At Dunton Green the branch line to Westerham struck off westwards, serving Chevening Halt, Brasted, and the delightful town of Westerham, even today a haven of tranquillity in the Kentish countryside. This is Chevening, photographed on 4 September 1960 with H class 0-4-4 tank 31533 about to leave, coupled to ex-LSWR corridor pull-push set 732. The direction of travel is not recorded, so we are unsure if the loco is about to head west (away from the camera) towards Brasted and Westerham or is propelling the set towards Dunton Green. The branch was one of the nearest rural byways to the London conurbation and had been put forward for electrification by the SECR when this was being planned in 1920. However, it was not included in the Southern's plan for electrification to reach Sevenoaks in 1935, and the line remained a steam worked branch until closure on 28 October 1961. Had electrification gone ahead, no doubt Westerham would have changed considerably in character. The locomotive was one of 66 members of the class and ran from July 1905 until September 1962 and was pull-push fitted in March 1960. The pull-push coaches began life in 1907 as LSWR emigrant corridor vehicles. These were built to a composite loading gauge to allow them to run over the Metropolitan widened lines (and to other restricted locations besides) and were shorter, narrower, and had slightly lower rooves than contemporary LSWR corridor coaches. Two nine coach trains of them were assembled (SR sets 473/74). They did not always run in this form, and in 1943 the coaches were rebuilt and reformed into nine two-coach pull-push sets; SR set numbers 731-739. In this form they lasted until 1960 and 1962. The tranquil surroundings of Chevening Halt have now changed beyond all recognition, and if the photographer were to stand here today, he would be in the middle of the A21/M25/M26 interchange and be deafened by the roar of constant traffic. *D. Clark 0752*

Above: On the Chatham main line 4-EPB unit S5115 enters Rochester on 10 May 1958 with a service to Gillingham, while L class 4-4-0 No 31781 stands in the down loop at the head of BR Mk 1 three coach set 530. A total of 213 of these 4-EPB (4-car Electro-Pneumatic Brake) units were completed for SR suburban services between 1951 and 1957. They were largely to the previous Bulleid 4-SUB design but were updated in terms of brakes, controls, couplings, and layout of driving cabs and so could not be used with earlier units. They could, however, be coupled to all later BR (Southern Region) slam door electric stock and some remained in service until 1995. Unit 5115 (by no means did they always carry an S prefix to the unit number) was formed in April 1954 with eight bay motor brakes S14229/30S at each end, with ten-compartment trailer S15193S and ten bay trailer S15243S between them. At least one of the underframes had seen previous service carrying rebuilt wooden bodywork in an earlier 3/4-SUB unit. No 5115 ran until October 1992, but by then had seen two changes of compartment trailer and would have been known then to railway staff as a class 415. There were eventually six sub-divisions to the class depending on whether they were SR built, BR built, in original formations, reformed, refurbished, or re-geared. It all got very complicated towards the end with many reformations and renumberings! *A. E. Bennett 3036*

Focus on Faversham

The next series of photographs were almost all taken at Faversham on Whit Monday 18 May 1959. This station was, and indeed still is, a major junction in East Kent where the former London, Chatham, and Dover Railway lines from the capital to Thanet and towards Canterbury and Dover diverge. The first two pictures are taken from the down end of the up-island platform, looking eastwards. Works for the forthcoming first stage of the Kent Coast electrification are nearing completion; the full electric service commencing just four weeks later 15 June. On the right may be seen the old LCDR Saxby & Farmer signal box (Faversham B), which dates from complete reconstruction of the station in 1898, together with the new box which will take over in just six days time from 24 May 1959 and which will control the new colour light signalling. Signal department staff are in attendance, even working over the bank holiday, such was the urgency by that time!

An unidentified Schools class 4-4-0 runs in with a train from Ramsgate to Victoria; the train reporting number 276 being clearly visible on the smoke box, with a slightly less clear chalked inscription above which says "3.32 VA". It gave the departure time from Ramsgate; no doubt provided for the benefit of the fellow who had the job of affixing these boards to the locomotives at their starting stations. These reporting numbers were regularly used to identify trains at busy periods for the benefit of the signalmen along the route; Bank Holidays in particular, when many additional trains were run. The train itself is composed of a restriction 1 SECR "Continental" brake third (now second class) to SR Diagram 164, followed by at least three Maunsell vehicles, after which the rest of the train disappears around the junction points from the direction of Whitstable, Herne Bay, and Margate. The final coach visible is a restriction 1 unclassed open saloon to SR Diagram 2653, a type previously more common on boat trains. *A. E. Bennett 4776*

The next train in; reporting number 277 (with the 3.28 VA Dover Priory departure time chalked on), arrives behind an unidentified U1 class mogul. This is formed of a nine coach Maunsell restriction 1 set: one of 217 or 218 most probably. Note the up-home signals at clear; and how far away from the up-Dover line they are situated, but lofty enough to be visible above any carriage stock stabled in the three sidings alongside the main line. Over in the downside yard are three departmental vehicles; no doubt being used by the staff carrying out the electrification works. They are a former LSWR Ironclad restaurant car (as a staff mess room), a LSWR covered van (for equipment) and a Signal & Telegraph utility workshop van. All would carry numbers prefixed DS. In the background may be seen the long lattice-constructed steel footbridge that spans the entire layout just east of the junction, and gave access to Faversham shed, which is hidden behind the arriving trains. *A. E. Bennett 4778*

We are now on the footbridge, looking back towards the junction points and Faversham station. Another unidentified Schools class leaves with the 12.26pm Chatham-Ramsgate service hauling Bulleid eight set 474 – one of two reformed and augmented BRCW three coach sets (the other was 473) assembled for Eastern Section Ramsgate services in 1954. As three sets they carried the numbers 803 and 804. On the extreme left is a pre-cast concrete hut; a product of the casting yard at Exmouth Junction, and clearly newly installed, while another is seen extreme right. A Standard Five is adjacent and a selection of ex-SECR locomotives stand behind a loco ash wagon immediately in front of the photographer. The locomotive shed is out of sight to the left while a small wagon repair shop is on the other side of the footbridge. On the right are some ballast wagons, including one of the SECR/ Leeds Forge Company hoppers of 1915 vintage, to SR Diagram 1746. Some of the later BR Herring, Trout and Dogfish wagons were similar. *A. E. Bennett 4768*

The photographer has now walked to the south end of the footbridge over the line to Canterbury and Dover, from which we see N1 class 2-6-0 No 31879 departing with another Maunsell restriction 1 set for Dover. The locomotive shed (code 73E) is seen to the right while the carriage sidings seen from the platform end in previous views are on the left, with a Maunsell restriction 4 set in road two. The precast concrete walkways giving easy access to the stock are new, as is the concrete trunking in the six-foot way and the new lighting masts, which will replace the earlier timber poles; one of which may be seen at extreme left. The conductor rails have yet to see regular use but testing of stock and crew training had almost certainly started. Beside the loco shed is a former LSWR gangwayed luggage van almost devoid of paint. Several LSWR 56ft corridor coaches were appropriated for ambulance car service during World War One and were returned to the railway in 1922. Most had been considerably modified and the expense of returning them to passenger use was unjustified, so they were converted into passenger brake vans instead. This example was previously SR No 345, withdrawn in April 1947 to become departmental van 447s, allocated to Faversham shed from March 1950 until July 1961. After electrification of the North Kent lines, Faversham shed continued to be used as a diesel depot. *A. E. Bennett 4770*

Taken just over a month earlier on 11 April 1959, we see ex-SECR C class 0-6-0 No 31256 being coaled outside the shed. One of 109 examples of the class built between 1900 and 1908, they were very much the workhorses of Kent and could be seen all over the South Eastern system, and much of the Southern as far west as Hampshire, until the early 1960s. No 31256 dates from June 1900 and put in just over 60 years' service before withdrawal in July 1961. In design, they owe a lot to the LCDR; indeed, some railwaymen and enthusiasts regarded them as a development of the Chatham B2 class goods and referred to them as B3's. Although the class is attributed to Harry Wainwright; Robert Surtees of the LCDR had a considerable hand in their design. One was rebuilt into a saddle tank for shunting at Richborough Port, then later at Bricklayers Arms, and one more was withdrawn in December 1947. All the rest became BR stock in 1948 and only one failed to receive its BR number. The final three survivors were Nos 31271/80 and 31592, which were retained as shunters at Ashford Wagon Works until as late as September 1967, when the latter was bought for preservation and may now be seen operating on the Bluebell Railway. On the day of the photograph, the carriage sidings on the far side of the Dover line are occupied by BR Mk 1 stock. *A. Swain E81-3*

For our last Faversham picture, we return to the station to see the prototype U1 class 2-6-0 No 31890 arriving with the 4.55pm Margate to Victoria service, comprising Maunsell restriction 4 eight-coach set 236. This locomotive began life as unique three-cylinder 2-6-4 tank A890 of class K1 in December 1925, however rough riding and excessive rolling at speed soon caused several minor derailments, and some redesign work had to be undertaken. Events soon overtook this with the derailment of two-cylinder River tank A800 north of Sevenoaks on 24 August 1927, resulting in the loss of 13 lives and a considerable number of other injuries. Consequently, both classes were taken out of service immediately, and were rebuilt as 2-6-0 tender locomotives. No A890 re-emerged from Ashford Works in June 1928 as a U1 but differed somewhat from the other twenty members of the class (No A891-1910), which followed in 1931. Most obvious are the raised footplate over the cylinders with a step down and the pairing of a flat-sided 3500-gallon tender. The class remained intact until late 1962, when all but four were withdrawn; leaving these four (including 31890) to run until mid-1963. By that time, the survivors were all on the Central section. Also visible beyond the station is probably the best reason why Faversham is well-known; the Shepherd Neame brewery and rather distinctive oast houses. They claim to be the oldest brewer in the country; established in 1698. In slightly more recent times, the company even had private-owner railway beer vans but today, of course, all their products travel by road. *A. E. Bennett 4780*

Top: Ramsgate at 7pm on 2 May 1961, and a view looking across the carriage cleaning shed beside the station towards the new electric stock maintenance depot being built alongside: more works for phases one and two of the Kent Coast electrification. Indeed, a closer look inside the carriage shed reveals the presence of a 4-CEP electric unit, as by now electric trains are serving Ramsgate from the Margate direction. The loco shed building (out of sight to the left) has already been incorporated into the new structure. Interim steam servicing arrangements are in force, which probably accounts for D1 No 31739 and N class mogul 31854 standing outside the carriage shed instead of in the loco yard. The D1's driver appears to be awaiting instructions from a shunter behind the mogul. The loco is fully coaled (well, coal of a sort!), so may be about to draw a set of carriages out of road four and propel them into the station; perhaps with a pilot engine at the far end. The head code on the mogul indicates that it will return to London via Canterbury West, Ashford, and Tonbridge. No 31854 was one of the earlier full front-end frame rebuilds, dating from August 1957, as indicated by the BR class four blast-pipe and chimney and curved frame extensions above the buffer beam. Already competent locomotives, this work enhanced their performance further and enabled a few to continue to serve until May 1966, although this example was scrapped in June 1964; by then allocated to Exmouth Junction shed. *D. Clark 0565*

Bottom: The same location but on 17 May 1960. The concrete block walls of the Southern locomotive shed may be seen with the new EMU maintenance structure; predictably of brick and corrugated asbestos sheet construction, clearly the risks of this wonder material were not appreciated then. D1 class 4-4-0 No 31489 looks most presentable, as does the coal on this occasion. Most of the loco sheds in East Kent took at least some of their supplies from the Kent coalfield; often carried in ex-Southern Railway 21-ton eight-plank mineral wagons of which a total of 989 were built in the 1930s. Unless one travelled to East Kent, they were a comparatively rare sight elsewhere. The D1 and E1 rebuilds were excellent machines and showed just what could be achieved by a judicious rebuilding. But, of course, the original D and E class locomotives were already basically sound machines anyway. What was once said about the making of a silk purse out of a sow's ear! *D. Clark 0883*

The up Golden Arrow departs from Dover at 6.13pm on 23 May 1959 behind Battle of Britain pacific 34085 *501 Squadron;* the third time we have seen this engine on the train, so clearly a Stewart's Lane favourite at this period. On the left is Archcliffe Junction signal box, which controls the junction between the lines to Dover Marine and round to Dover Priory, the junction itself is just behind where the photographer is standing. The box was a Southern Railway replacement for an earlier structure and opened in June 1928. Beside the box is the former military platform, later used as a staff halt; today occupied by vans. The starting signal for this platform is the bracket-mounted one immediately right of the box. Notice the C marked signal just above the Pullman cars. This is a calling-on arm, used when the road to which the upper arm refers is partly occupied, and therefore a warning to locomotive crews to proceed with caution and to expect to find vehicles standing somewhere along that line. If the road was fully clear to the next signal, then the home arm above would be pulled off. On the right a C class goods and a BR standard 4-6-0 stand alongside the coaling plant on Dover shed. The Arrow has the usual four-wheeled utility van at the head, followed by one of the two SR Diagram 1106 conflat Ds reserved for the four Customs-sealed baggage-box containers that would be craned onto or off the ship as part of the London-Paris service. These two vehicles were renumbered S4207/8 in the van stock list between April 1950 and February 1961 and were repainted crimson lake, later SR green to reflect their upgraded passenger-rated status. These colours were limited to the side rails only. After 1961, they reverted to their former goods-rated identities as Diagram 1383 wagons S39582 and S39614. The usual bogie luggage van seen in previous views of the train would now, of course, be at the rear. *A. E. Bennett 4809*

We now start to return eastwards and the next location is Folkestone Junction on 15 April 1961. Rebuilt Battle of Britain No 34088 *213 Squadron* is departing with an up-boat train for Victoria: 12 very mixed coaches and a luggage van at the front. The first coach is a Maunsell restriction 1 unclassed open brake to Diagram 2654, followed by another restriction 1 vehicle; this time a corridor first, then a BR Mk 1 open second followed by a Bulleid and then more Maunsell restriction 4 vehicles. A typical boat train formation of the period, and one of about ten or 11 listed in carriage working notices at that time. The whole train is being given a helping shove by an ex-GWR pannier tank at the rear, which had (probably with two others) previously brought the train up from Folkestone Harbour over the lines upon which the photographer is standing. Electrification is now just two months away and reconstruction work is well advanced, with some colour light signals, conductor rails in place and new carriage access walkways and overhead lighting gantries erected. In fact, the juice went live a little before 12 June and the writer spent a disappointing morning observing trains here in late May 1961 to find that the only steam-hauled service seen was the down Arrow behind Appledore at 12.25pm. Almost all other services were in the hands of Sulzers, Cromptons and the new malachite green electric locomotives, even if the stock was still loco-hauled coaches. *D. Clark 0493*

Ashford shed yard, on 7 May 1961. Visible are Crompton D6501 on the left, then C class 0-6-0 31684, ex-works U class mogul 31807 with another C and N1 mogul behind, N class 31854 immediately ahead, BR standard 2 tank 84026 and two Schools class 4-4-0s on the right. Just seen inside the shed building is rebuilt WC 34014 *Budleigh Salterton,* then a Bricklayers Arms engine. This was slightly unusual, as Ashford seldom had any pacifics on its strength, although a couple of original BBs were briefly allocated there between 1959 and 1961. No 31807 has just completed a general overhaul, which took place between 29 March and 29 April and looks ready to return to its home shed 75B at Redhill. It would make one further move: to Norwood Junction in December 1962, before withdrawal in January 1964. The presence of a BR standard 2 tank was not unusual here, as the final ten completed (Nos 84020-29) were allocated to Ashford between 1957 and 1961. They were used especially on the local services across Romney Marsh to Rye and Hastings and north from Ashford towards Canterbury and Ramsgate but could also be seen on other lines in East Kent. None survive, but the Bluebell Railway is rebuilding No 84030 using similar class 2 2-6-0 tender locomotive No 78059 as a basis. When purchased from Barry scrapyard the locomotive was without a tender and this, plus the fact that the tank engine version of the class had Southern Region associations, helped the buyers arrive at this course of action. The ten-road shed building still looks in good order. It was built in 1931 using pre-cast concrete parts from Exmouth Junction, but appearances may be deceptive, since after closure in 1962 it was occupied for a time by the South Eastern Steam Centre preservation group, and by then some parts of the structure had been demolished due to deterioration. However, despite the centre holding regular open days in the early 1970s, financial difficulties eventually forced its closure in 1976, and the whole area has now been redeveloped. *D. Clark 0617*

Opposite Top: Ashford regularly saw ex-LBSCR classes for overhaul after Brighton Works closed for the first time in the early 1930s. Although it reopened, staff time was concentrated mostly on new-build rather than overhauls during the war. Here, on 7 May 1961, is C2X No 32546 from 75C: Norwood Junction. Presumably, it was in for works attention, not that any was given. These 0-6-0 locomotives dated from 1893 and 1902 and were originally built as class C2; a total of 55 being completed to the design of Robert Billinton. When built, they were quite adequate for the Brighton's goods traffic but within a few years, something more powerful was required. Douglas Earle Marsh was by then in charge at Brighton and his initial answer was his larger C3 goods engine. However, in the words of enginemen these could not pull the skin off a rice pudding, so the C2 class was looked at again. By marrying a modified C3 boiler to the C2 chassis and cylinders a perfectly successful heavy-duty 0-6-0 resulted and no less than 45 engines of the class were rebuilt into C2X between 1908 and 1940. No 546 began life in January 1902 and was rebuilt as seen here in June 1912. It had probably arrived here having been proposed for works by Norwood shed staff, but on examination it was not deemed worthy of overhaul and was condemned in April 1961. So, despite a full load of coal in the tender, the locomotive has worked its final duty. The last members of the class were finally broken up at Ashford in February 1962. *D. Clark 0616*

Bottom: Across the Dover main line from the shed was Ashford Works, where L1 class 4-4-0 No 31759 is seen awaiting its fate on 7 May 1961. Fifteen of these were built early in 1926 by North British Locomotive Company in something of a hurry, to supply the urgent need for increased power on Kent Coast trains. They were a Maunsell development of the SECR L class plus an amalgam of what had been done with the D1/E1 rebuilds a few years earlier. Like those classes, they had a more-than-passing resemblance to Midland 4-4-0s but were rather better performers. This was largely due to the influence of Ashford's then chief draughtsman; James Clayton, whom Maunsell had recruited from Derby Works in 1914. Despite the subsequent appearance of more modern classes, they proved successful and continued to work on South Eastern lines until 1961. They were particularly useful on the Chatham main line, as this still had weight restriction issues in the 1920s and were often allocated to Bricklayers Arms and Dover sheds. Four of the class migrated to Eastleigh between 1952 and 1954, but otherwise they seldom left Kent until phase one of the electrification scheme went live in June 1959. No 31759 has probably already worked its last duty, as withdrawal took place in November 1961. A few then moved to Nine Elms and were used briefly on SW section services: the writer recalls seeing the final survivor, No 31786, shunting vans at Woking in early 1962. *D. Clark 0615*

A rural Kentish byway: indeed, it would be difficult to think of a more rural railway line in the south east than the Kent and East Sussex. Tenterden Town station, possibly in early 1934; we do not have an exact date, but this seems to fit the available evidence as the locomotive KESR No 4 (ex-LSWR Beattie saddle tank No 335) ran on the line from 1932, until laid aside in October 1946. The loco was eventually broken up at Ashford Works in August 1948. The carriage at the rear of the train, KESR No 10, is probably the most interesting relic, and was last known to have been used in July 1936. Reputed to be an LSWR Royal saloon of 1851, built following a request by Queen Victoria for a carriage for use by her children, it was a first-class coupe; with a wide compartment in the middle and a half-compartment (coupe) at each end; presumably with seats facing outward in each instance. There were originally three doors on each side. It measured about 19ft long and just under 8ft wide. Its last recorded LSWR use was on the Weymouth and Portland branch in 1909. Eventually purchased by Col. H. F. Stephens around 1912, it appeared on the Kent & East Sussex Railway, and by the 1930s the interior had been much altered, such that there were just two interconnecting compartments; one small and one large, accessed by one central door on each side. It was reputed to be the only coach on the railway that had working lights, so was used on all evening trains until final withdrawal in 1936. A note in 'The Railway Magazine' for 1937 states that the coach had been acquired by the Southern Railway and had turned up at Ashford, and that it was intended for a new museum being set up at Eastleigh. Several other interesting relics were also collected for this museum, but with the onset of war most were regrettably broken up for scrap instead. However, coach No 10 was sold off, and its body grounded at Dunsfold in Surrey, where it remained until finally burnt sometime in the late 1950s. What a shame that it did not survive. The late Denis Cullum: the indefatigable Southern carriage enthusiast, certainly found it and recorded the location in woodland alongside the Dunsfold-Plaistow Road. The other coach is an ex-Great Eastern Railway brake third, KESR No 20. The Kent & East Sussex Railway, along with all the other Colonel Stephens light railway empire, managed to avoid the Grouping in 1923 and only entered the BR fold in 1948. Inevitable closure of the line to passengers took place in January 1954, but the section between Tenterden and Robertsbridge remained open for goods traffic until 1961. This enabled the preservation movement to marshal its forces in readiness to take over as BR moved out. By good fortune, the line remains with us today as a popular tourist attraction. *Dr I. C. Allen 68*

The next rural branch line westwards ran from the SER main line at Paddock Wood up into the Kentish Weald to terminate at Hawkhurst; well, almost. In fact, the terminus was located over a mile north of the village at Gill's Green, on high ground which made the prospect of extending southwards difficult, although an extension to Tenterden and Rye was proposed at one time. Here we see a view of Hawkhurst station forecourt on 14 August 1955; the occasion of an RCTS rail tour visit (The Wealden Limited), and a SECR Continental corridor third coach may be seen in the main platform while the branch train: LBSCR pull-push set 721 occupies the bay platform on the right. Motive power along the branch was provided by H class 31177 and O1 class 31048 but several other locomotives were used on other parts of the tour, which began and ended at Victoria. The stock was an eight-coach formation of two Maunsell narrow Hastings brake coaches, five SECR Continental corridor thirds and Pullman buffet car 183. Apart from the Hastings line Pullman car, the rest were part of restriction 0 ten-coach set 938. The station building was built in 1893 in timber and corrugated iron, much in the style of Colonel H. F. Stephens, who was resident engineer on the construction of the line, and the layout at the terminus was made to facilitate any future extension southwards. This was never to be, and the line continued in relative obscurity until closure on 11 June 1961. Goods traffic receipts far outweighed passenger revenue, and the only time that stations were crowded were when rail tours or hop-pickers descended on the line, the latter particularly between August and October. A smart-looking Ford Prefect stands on the approach road; registered in London in that year. These popular family cars were built between 1953 and 1961. *L. R. Freeman 2064*

Quintessentially Kent: complete with oast houses! C class No 31256 hauls ex-SECR pull-push set 656 into Goudhurst on 10 June 1961: a day before closure of the branch. The attractive signal box may be seen and notice that both platforms are signalled to allow departures towards Cranbrook and Hawkhurst. Indeed, two months later and everything remained in-situ, enabling the writer to operate the signals from the box; the source of much boyhood pleasure! Others must have done the same, as on his next visit the box had been securely boarded up and the signal wires disconnected. The line remained untouched for some time, and demolition only took place during 1964. A vintage Morris van waits at the crossing before continuing its journey along the A262, while the village is a good mile behind the cameraman, at higher altitude too. It is well worth a visit, and claims to be the prettiest village in Kent, boasting more than 200 listed buildings. Regrettably, few came to visit by train. *R. Hobbs 2488*

The other branch coming in to Paddock Wood; this time from the north, was the SER line from Strood along the Medway Valley through Maidstone West. This was electrified as far as Maidstone in 1939, leaving the steam-worked branch service southwards to Paddock Wood and onwards to Tonbridge until full electrification from 12 June 1961. An H Class, No 31308, arriving at East Farleigh on 3 June 1961, with a train bound for Tonbridge. The photographer is standing on the footbridge, and the other platform is behind him on the opposite side of the level crossing, a very common arrangement on South Eastern lines. Some stations did not even have the footbridge for safe passenger access: one just used the road crossing! The timber clap-board construction was also a characteristic feature of SER stations; indeed, it was a common way of building throughout Kent. The goods yard and goods shed have already been taken out of use. The train formation is interesting; a Maunsell restriction 4 corridor third (now second), a restriction 0 corridor composite, a 1936 open third (now second) and an LMS brake coach on the rear. Perhaps the notorious 30-year rule has taken effect and the former Maunsell brake in the set was older than this threshold and has had to be withdrawn from traffic; leaving the staff with a train of passenger-carrying vehicles but no accommodation for the guard, or way to operate hand and emergency braking. Those giving out the edict did not always realise that SR carriage sets might be formed of coaches of varying ages, so if the instruction was carried out to the letter, it left an imbalance of stock types with which to form the trains. *A. E. Bennett 5570*

While journeying briefly down the Medway valley, we stop at Maidstone West, where Bulleid Q1 class 0-6-0 No 33034 stands in the still-busy yard on 7 April 1956. Much has been written about these unconventional-looking locomotives but, despite appearances, they were conventional 0-6-0s beneath that austerity clothing; extremely powerful and shorn of all unnecessary frills. Indeed, their haulage power could sometimes be their undoing as adhesive weight available for braking was limited and so, while they could pull a heavy goods train with ease, stopping it within a reasonable distance was another matter. Bulleid's argument would be that all goods trains should be fully vacuum-braked; but of course, they were not. A varied selection of wagons is visible, including examples from BR, the LMS and LNER, but nothing GWR or Southern. It was not unusual to find a Southern goods train with not a single Southern wagon in it; perhaps only the brake van, but SR wagons only made up a small proportion of the total British Railways stock and once they were distributed the length and breadth of the country, it must be admitted that they could be rare birds. Note also the old South Eastern double water crane at the end of the platform, with the barley twist lamp post in front. Evidence of electrification comes with the eight-coach stopping marker mounted on the lamp post. *A. E. Bennett 1128*

Opposite Top: We return to Paddock Wood to continue our journey up the South Eastern main line. Here, we are looking down the main line through the 1893 station in the direction of Ashford on 6 May 1961. C class No 31716 is leaving for Tonbridge with a Maunsell pull-push set. The fact that the loco is not pull-push fitted will not matter and the train may have started its journey at Maidstone West and entered the station across the junction just seen under the footbridge. The station layout is evident, with two through lines, two passing loops alongside the platforms and down-facing bays on either side. A small up-side goods yard is seen on the right, but the extensive sidings on the down side have already gone and a new building is in the process of being erected by contractor Laing; with what looks like an old flour mill building beyond. Later, this became the site for a Transfesa rail-served Continental freight depot. Also seen is the lofty east yard signal cabin; astride the line coming in from Hawkhurst. BR Mk 1 3-set 555 and an H class locomotive are at the down platform, but they will not be going anywhere just yet, as the down through signals are off for an express to pass. On the left is a BR Mk 1 full brake in lined maroon livery while the old cattle dock (seen above the C class) has already been taken out of use and platform extension is taking place. In the foreground is an old LSWR van, now in departmental use. *D. Clark 0582*

Bottom: Moving down to track level on the same day, we see Schools class 30934 *St Lawrence* departing from the up platform with a train for London Bridge that started at Ramsgate and travelled via Canterbury West and Ashford. The locomotive is one of those fitted with a Lemaitre blast pipe and chimney by Oliver Bulleid in 1939. Half of the class were so equipped but, unlike the Lord Nelsons that were similarly fitted, it did not have much effect. The Schools class were already excellent performers, so it might be argued that the expense was unjustified. It did not necessarily improve their appearance, either. No 30934 was an Ashford engine and does not look well cared for, but will no doubt put in a good performance uphill from Tonbridge to Knockholt. The train crew are clearly aware of the photographer's presence. Bulleid four-set 88 forms the train. A Southern pillbox 25-ton brake van occupies the sidings and note the rather unusual, interlaced point work at the entrance to the up-side yard. This seems to be a feature at several ex-SER stations. *D. Clark 0600*

Above: Our last picture at Paddock Wood features another Lemaitre-fitted Schools class, but this time arriving at the up platform on a rather miserable 3 April 1961 (Easter Monday, so typical Bank Holiday weather!), timed at 10.23am. Note that this is the same train, duty and stock seen in the picture at Polhill signal box on 1 July 1960 (DC1015) but this time may be more easily identified as the 8.34am Hastings-Tonbridge via Ashford (depart 9.30am), which should have left Paddock Wood at 10.10am. The locomotive is wrongly identified as No 30934, but this time the allocation is Bricklayers Arms, so it is more likely to be 30931 *Kings Wimbledon* instead. Over on the left, in the Maidstone West branch bay (platform four) stands an SECR pull-push set; possibly No 656 which was a regular over the Hawkhurst branch. The Hawkhurst bay (platform one) may just be seen on the right. *D. Clark 2004*

The combination of a class 33 and a class 24 diesel was not unknown on the South Eastern section between 1960 and 1962. Passing Tonbridge at 3.30pm on 2 April 1960, we see such a combination with brand new Crompton D6501 piloting Sulzer D5012 on a train of Pullman cars. This might look like the Arrer stock but the fact that no headboard or even a head code is displayed points to a test run or empty stock. In fact, the combination had worked this all-Pullman boat train down to Dover via Chatham earlier in the day and is simply on the return journey via Tonbridge. Maybe it is also a crew training trip and doubling up as a test-run with the Sulzer just adding to the load? On the down run it was almost certainly there to provide steam heating. The platforms are deserted, and this was unusual when the Golden Arrow passed: staff would turn out to see the event, if nothing else. The writer recalls such occasions at Ashford and Folkestone Junction in 1960 and 1961 with plenty of staff and enthusiasts watching, but when he saw the Arrow pass through Tonbridge in 1972, just before the final run, not a soul looked up. By then the class 71 electric locomotive and stock were all in blue/blue and grey corporate livery, with only three Pullmans, and so did not look much different from any other Kent Coast service. *D. Clark 1255*

A down Dover boat train comes through Tonbridge on 18 October 1959 with original Battle of Britain pacific 34068 *Kenley* in charge; Stewart's Lane duty one – so this will be the 8.30am from Victoria, due at Tonbridge around an hour later. *Kenley* was one of the early Bulleid withdrawals, in December 1963, from Salisbury shed. The stock is one of the nine South Eastern boat train formations listed in the carriage working notices; with a Maunsell restriction 1 unclassed open brake on the front, followed by four BR Mk 1 open seconds, then two Pullman cars cut into the rake, followed by at least three Bulleids beyond; probably with a utility van on the rear. One BR Mk 1 open second has been removed as the CWN calls for five to be included; but we are now well into October and demand may be reducing. Maunsell restriction 1 four-car set 182 stands in the down through platform: probably on a local service towards Ashford. Conductor rail pots are already in place on the up lines and the new conductor rails may be seen dumped ready in the four-foot of the up main. *R. Hobbs 1457*

Oxted station, just after 9am on 28 September 1961. H class No 31533 arrived in the up-platform to connect with a London service and would have crossed to the down line and shunted into the down bay (out of view on the right) to await the arrival of the 8.01 London Bridge-Tunbridge Wells West via East Grinstead train. This has now departed, leaving a bogie van B in the platform, to which No 31533 and pull-push set 663 have coupled and are now leaving for Tunbridge Wells via Ashurst at 9.04am. The van worked a cycle, starting at London Bridge at 3.27am the day before, travelling to Three Bridges. It then went by goods train to Forest Row, and back to East Grinstead. On the following day, it set out on the 6.34am to London Bridge, down on the 8.01 and 9.04 as seen here, then quickly transferred to the 9.40am van train onwards to Tonbridge. Next, it moved on to Redhill, leaving Tonbridge at 10.35am, where it would almost certainly convey mail to the busy sorting office adjacent to the down platform. Finally, it would be picked up at 5.32pm by an up Brighton-London Bridge van train and be able to start the cycle all over again the following day. In theory, two vans could alternate the service, but any other van B might be substituted at this point in the cycle. The Croydon, Oxted and East Grinstead Railway was a joint LBSCR/SER venture dating from 1884 and the route left the Brighton main line at South Croydon, passing south-eastwards through Warlingham and Oxted to East Grinstead and Eridge, where it connected with the LBSCR lines to Tunbridge Wells and Uckfield, while connection to the South Eastern's Redhill-Tonbridge line was made via the Crowhurst spur. For this reason, both LBSCR and SECR locomotives and trains could be seen through Oxted. *L. R. Freeman 6697*

Rails around Redhill

Redhill is a strategically placed junction on the London-Brighton main line, where the former South Eastern's cross-country route from Reading through Guildford, and onwards to Tonbridge joins and leaves again. The station has been an important interchange since the late 1840s and was operated jointly by both the LBSCR and the South Eastern Railway and was known as Redhill Junction until after the Grouping. Indeed, before the SER opened their cut-off line northwards from Tonbridge to London through Sevenoaks and Orpington in 1868, most South Eastern trains to Kent passed through the station. Ex-LBSCR non-stop trains ceased to pass through the station in 1899, when the Quarry avoiding line was completed, easing congestion. Nevertheless, the station has remained a bottleneck, and difficult to operate. This has only recently been relieved by the construction of an additional platform (numbered rather unusually as platform zero) on the western side of the existing lines. The existing platforms one, two and three have each been sub-divided into 1A, 1B, etc., allowing two shorter trains to be dealt with simultaneously.

The strategic importance of Redhill was acknowledged during World War Two as one of several wartime control centres set up; other Southern ones were at Orpington, Woking, and Southampton. In addition, the Southern purchased Deepdene House at Dorking for use as wartime administration headquarters, so Redhill was handily placed for that, too. It was also far enough away from the centre of London to avoid disruption by bombing. We will now take an extended look at each route into the junction, as well as some views around the station itself and the nearby locomotive shed, as largely seen through the camera of Roy Hobbs: a local Reigate resident.

Opposite Top: A sylvan setting for rebuilt West Country No 34014 *Budleigh Salterton* hauling a utility van and a Bulleid set, and heading westwards towards Redhill at Bough Beech, just east of Edenbridge at 5.41pm on 14 May 1960. Few services over the line from Tonbridge to Redhill saw Bulleid pacifics, as SECR classes and SR moguls were very much the staple of the area. This is the 2.45pm from Margate to Cannon Street, which was routed via the old SER main line through Tonbridge and Redhill, and not a train to choose if you were in a hurry! The photographer's trusty bicycle can be seen propped against the fence on the right. Bough Beech may be better known today as a 285-acre reservoir built between 1968 and 1969, just north of the location seen here and owned by Sutton & East Surrey Water Company; an amalgamation of at least eight smaller local water concerns. Two medieval buildings had to be removed from the site to build the reservoir, and part of one of them, Winkhurst Farm, has been re-erected at the Weald and Downland Museum at Singleton, West Sussex, where it is known as Winkhurst Tudor Kitchen. The reservoir was for some time designated a local nature reserve where, amongst other birds, Ospreys are regularly sighted on their Spring and Autumn migrations. *D. Clark 0881*

Opposite Bottom: A general view of Redhill shed, looking north from The Mound on a rather dull day in 1958. This gives a good idea of the topography, with Redhill station out of sight in the right background; the eight-car formation of 2-HAL/BIL electric units are leaving and are heading down the hill behind the coaling stage towards Earlswood to join the Quarry line with a semi-fast service to Three Bridges and beyond. On the extreme right, the Tonbridge line curves away, and a diesel shunter is moving a brake van on the down South Eastern line into or out of the down yard even further right, with the goods shed visible beyond it. Left of centre, above the coal stage, the line towards Reigate, Guildford, and Reading curves away westwards, with the up goods yard beyond that. The western fringes of Redhill town climb away behind. From here, it is obvious that any cross-country service from west to east (and vice-versa) must run into the station and reverse out again; crossing the Brighton lines as it does so; almost invariably changing engines in the process. Unseen, the Quarry avoiding line burrows underneath where the cameraman is standing, thus obviating non-stop Brighton line trains having to pass through Redhill station. Before this was completed in 1899, the congested state of the station was a considerable source of friction between the LBSCR and the SER. The shed itself was a South Eastern structure dating from 1853 and was re-roofed by BR in the usual corrugated asbestos sheeting in 1950. Locomotives visible include an ex-LSWR 700 class (seen in the next picture), N and N1 class moguls, an ex-LBSCR C2X, Schools, BR standard 4 tank and possibly an LMS Black 5 behind the C2X. The shed regularly saw ex-GWR locomotives that worked in from Reading, as well as more occasional LMS and LNER visitors. It was destined to be the Central section's last steam depot and closed finally in June 1965; although occasional steam visitors continued to call for a little while longer. *R. Hobbs 1012*

At the back of Redhill shed, we see ex-LSWR 700 class 0-6-0 goods No 30326 more closely, having arrived on a ballast train, maybe from Guildford, where the locomotive was allocated. The date is 1958. The loco appears cold and out of steam, so either had no booked return working or had failed in the vicinity and was awaiting attention. The thirty members of this class date from 1897 and were Dugald Drummond's answer to the South Western's need for heavy goods engines. In their original form, and numbered 687-716 on the South Western, they were like previous engines designed by Drummond when he was in the employ of the Caledonian Railway. Once run-in, they proved their worth but in time the traffic outpaced their capabilities, and it fell to Drummond's successor, Robert Urie, to modify them, including extending the smoke box, superheating, and repositioning the boiler some nine inches higher. The result, which was a similar transformation to the T9 4-4-0s, gave the LSWR a modern heavy 0-6-0 capable of hauling all but the heaviest main line goods trains. All thirty were rebuilt between 1920 and 1929, and this enabled them all to remain in service until 1957. The first withdrawal was because of collision damage, rather than a lack of employment for the class. Some renumbering took place in LSWR days and No 30326 was, in fact, built at LSWR No 708, becoming 326 a year after construction, and was rebuilt into the form seen here in June 1923. Withdrawal came in February 1962 and breaking up took place at Ashford Works: one of three of the class to be dealt with there. *R. Hobbs 1011*

Looking in the other direction, we see L class 4-4-0 No 31780 arriving with a train from Tonbridge, comprising a Maunsell restriction 0 three-set in rather grubby crimson lake and cream livery. No wonder the Southern Region was anxious to return to green livery after June 1956. The 22 examples of the L class were delivered concurrently with the outbreak of World War One and came from two suppliers: Beyer Peacock in Manchester and, somewhat ironically, A. Borsig of Berlin. Fortunately, those from Germany arrived before the declaration of war, but it meant that Borsig's were not paid for their work until May 1920! The locomotives were a Harry Wainwright design but modified somewhat by Richard Maunsell who took over as CME at Ashford just before the orders were placed. No 31780 was the penultimate member of the Borsig order and entered service in July 1914, running until July 1961. Until 1951 they were rarely seen outside Kent or East Sussex; usually no further west than Brighton, but ten of the class migrated to Eastleigh for use on local services between December 1951 and December 1952. The first withdrawals took place in 1956 and the final survivors, No. 31768/ 71, were withdrawn from Nine Elms in December 1961. In April 1960, the Southern Region made tentative plans to preserve No 31763, together with a former SECR boat train coach, but in those days money for preservation was scarce and the project failed. Behind the train the former South Eastern's marshalling yard can be seen, together with a Tonbridge-bound freight standing on the down line: possibly the train that the diesel shunter was shunting the brake van to or from in a previous picture. Perhaps the loco at the front has uncoupled and drawn forward out of sight before setting back into the yard to pick up some more wagons. *R. Hobbs 1013*

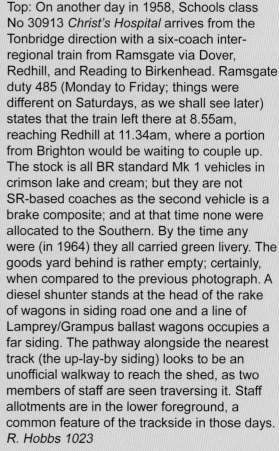

Top: On another day in 1958, Schools class No 30913 *Christ's Hospital* arrives from the Tonbridge direction with a six-coach inter-regional train from Ramsgate via Dover, Redhill, and Reading to Birkenhead. Ramsgate duty 485 (Monday to Friday; things were different on Saturdays, as we shall see later) states that the train left there at 8.55am, reaching Redhill at 11.34am, where a portion from Brighton would be waiting to couple up. The stock is all BR standard Mk 1 vehicles in crimson lake and cream; but they are not SR-based coaches as the second vehicle is a brake composite; and at that time none were allocated to the Southern. By the time any were (in 1964) they all carried green livery. The goods yard behind is rather empty; certainly, when compared to the previous photograph. A diesel shunter stands at the head of the rake of wagons in siding road one and a line of Lamprey/Grampus ballast wagons occupies a far siding. The pathway alongside the nearest track (the up-lay-by siding) looks to be an unofficial walkway to reach the shed, as two members of staff are seen traversing it. Staff allotments are in the lower foreground, a common feature of the trackside in those days. *R. Hobbs 1023*

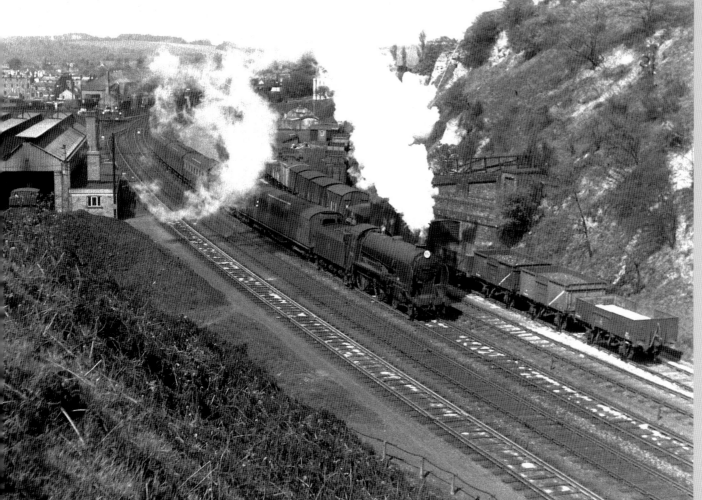

Bottom: The Birkenhead again, but this time going in the other direction on a rather sunnier weekday in 1958. Schools class 30912 *Downside* has duty 485 on this occasion and is departing eastwards at 2.38pm for Margate but will now travel via Ashford and Canterbury West instead of the longer route via Dover. Arrival at Margate is scheduled for 4.46pm. The train left Birkenhead at 7.35am, so a long day travelling for anyone making the full journey. Six Maunsell coaches; five in green, with an open third (now second) in blood and custard; whether there is a restaurant car as the second vehicle is not clear. The Brighton portion of the train will follow this out, down the main line towards Earlswood, behind an L class 4-4-0 from Tonbridge shed (duty No 293). The rather curiously shaped brick abutment behind Downside is a retaining wall and ventilation shaft above the mouth of Redhill tunnel, where the Quarry line dives underneath the Tonbridge route; the line passing diagonally across the photograph at this point. The entrance to the wartime control rooms was just behind the steam from the locomotive. *R. Hobbs 1032*

A more mundane 1958 service to Tonbridge leaves Redhill behind H class tank No 31259, passing the same location as the previous photograph. Set 423 is of interest; it should be a nine-coach formation of Maunsell Thanet restriction 1 vehicles, but only three are seen here: a brake third (now second, of course), a corridor composite and a corridor third (second), followed by two SR utility vans. The Thanet stock were the first new carriage designs completed by the newly formed Southern Railway beween1924 and 1925 to provide some much-needed corridor coaches on the lines out to North Kent. They were ordered as nine eight-coach trains plus five loose composites. They did not remain in these formations for very long as soon there were some four, seven, eight and nine-coach formations to be seen, often with one or two Pullman cars cut into the trains as required. In later years, they constituted SR sets 388, 423-425 and 460-463. One of these sets was involved in the Sevenoaks derailment with River tank No A800, causing the loss not only of 13 lives, but also of three Thanet coaches. Three more were lost in the Catford derailment of September 1946, while another was burnt out at Swanley Junction in March 1938. They were a singularly unlucky group of vehicles. *R. Hobbs 1026*

A view of the shed, taken from beside the Tonbridge line; showing the northern end of the building. Not so many pictures were taken looking in this direction. A selection of locomotives is visible, including an S15 4-6-0; probably No 30835, E4 radial tank No 32515, L class No 31766 and C class No 31244, giving some idea of the variety of motive power that could be seen on a regular basis. The S15s were allocated here relatively late; from 1951 and were usually those that were paired with six-wheeled tenders, Nos 833-837. They saw service on the Central section from 1936 onwards, allocated to either Brighton or New Cross Gate sheds. The E4's pottered around on local goods turns but were occasionally used on Reading or Tonbridge passenger trains; often when one of the turntables was out of action for repairs. The substantial rail-built inner home signals apply to trains coming in from Tonbridge and the arms refer to (from left to right) Tonbridge to up through, Tonbridge to up local (platform two), Tonbridge to up loop (platform one) and Tonbridge to up goods loop line: the one with the cross on it, so not yet in use. This end of the gantry was new to accommodate the arm; in the original print a lighter section of metalwork is just discernible. The exit from the lay-by siding was controlled by a ground disc signal, not seen in the picture. The wooden notice board reminds staff of the dangers of crossing the line. This is the way to access the shed from the station end; but it sure isn't very legible! *R. Hobbs 1039*

The LBSCR was fond of radial (0-6-2) tanks and after a solitary Stroudley F class prototype of 1891 (later reclassified as an E3), his successor Robert Billinton produced four classes of them between 1894 and 1905, as follows:

E3 class, known as small radials, with 4ft 6in driving wheels.   16 examples.
E4 class, known as large radials, with 5ft 0in driving wheels.   75 examples.
E5 class, a larger version of the E4 with 5ft 6in driving wheels.   30 examples.
E6 class, a larger version of the E3 with 4ft 6in driving wheels.   12 examples.

Subsequently, a few examples of each class, except the E3, were rebuilt with larger C2X type boilers, becoming E4X, E5X and E6X respectively. All except the Stroudley prototype of classes E3 and E4 received extended smokeboxes over a protracted period between 1912 and 1949. Those with larger wheels were intended for passenger work, while the 4ft 6in locos were essentially goods engines. In later years, all could be found working goods trains. The E4s were by far the most numerous and the longest lasting; four made it to 1963. No 32515 is seen at the rear of Redhill shed in August 1958 and looks rather more presentable than when seen in the previous picture. Built in April 1901, as LBSCR 515; named Swanmore, the locomotive put in 60 years' service, being withdrawn in May 1961. The shed allocation displayed (75A) is Brighton, but the engine seems to have spent most of its final years at Redhill. Just one member of the class survives in preservation: No 473, on the Bluebell Railway. Behind, S15 No 30835 lurks inside the shed. Note, too, the water tank mounted on the hillside beyond and the rather makeshift supply pipe down to the depot. No water pressure head problems here! *R. Hobbs 1024*

The coal stage and turntable at Redhill were to the south-west of the shed building; alongside the line descending towards Earlswood. Both were rebuilt by the Southern Railway and the new turntable was one of the largest on the Southern; with a nominal diameter of 65ft and capable of turning all Southern classes. Here we see double dome fitted C2X No 32527 about to be turned, with coal wagons standing on the raised coal road behind. Several of the Brighton classes acquired double domes; used to house the boiler top-feed arrangements, and a system favoured by Lawson Billinton; the last LBSCR locomotive superintendent. Most of the members of the C2X class carried them at various times over the years; even when top feed gave way to the more usual side-feed and the second dome was often left undisturbed. No 527 dates from September 1900 as a C2, being rebuilt as late as October 1939, and running until November 1960. These engines could be seen all over the Brighton system and, once boiler mountings were cut down slightly, they also appeared on former South Eastern routes. They were less commonly found on the South Western section, where crews did not appreciate them so much. The BR power code was 2F; supplemented by a Southern Region sub-classification A, hence the code 2FA over the number. There was similarly a sub-code B (i.e., 2FB) and other similar sub-codes A or B could be noted on the cab sides of some of the moguls and on Bulleid light pacifics. *R. Hobbs 1046*

Named Southern engines were a slightly more unusual occurrence at Redhill shed and were usually confined to the Schools class or, less often, the four Ashford-based King Arthurs. Here in early 1958, we seen N15 No 30802 *Sir Durnore* from 74A Ashford in company with a local N class mogul. The Knight has probably arrived with either a freight or an inter-regional train from the Tonbridge direction, but as no head code discs or duty number are displayed, we cannot say more. This engine was one of the final batches of the class, built in 1926 at Eastleigh Works and used mostly on the Central section until electrification. These were paired with somewhat ill-matching 3,500 gallon six-wheeled tenders; perfectly adequate for Central and South Eastern section duties, while most on the South Western section ran with 4,000-gallon bogie tenders. In June 1958 No 30802 received a bogie tender from Urie Arthur No 30750 and was soon re-allocated to Eastleigh. Withdrawal took place in July 1961, with a credited mileage of 1,096,024. Note that the signal with a cross upon the arm, seen in a general view of the shed earlier, has not yet been added. To accommodate that, the signal platform had to be extended at the left-hand end. *R. Hobbs 1082*

Stored locomotives became a feature of Redhill in the later days of steam and here we have D1 class No 31247 and L1 class No 31784 out of use at the back of the shed on 18 October 1959. There was another stored L1 on the next road, behind No 31247. By now, phase one of the Kent Coast electrification had been completed and there was an excess of motive power on the South Eastern section; particularly of 4-4-0 classes, and some of these were transferred (on paper at least) to South Western section sheds, including Nine Elms. In fact, many of the engines went into store at such locations as Feltham and Redhill, never to work again. No 31247 was built as SECR D class No 247 in April 1903 by Dubs & Company of Glasgow, rebuilt as a D1 in April 1921 and was reallocated to Nine Elms from Stewart's Lane (so it only moved a mile or so by road, but an awful lot further by rail!) in June 1959 and may have been used there for a few weeks before being rusticated to Redhill. It was finally withdrawn in July 1961. No 31784 was built by the North British Locomotive Company (Dubs successors) in April 1926 and was also transferred to Nine Elms in June 1959, but from Dover shed. It, too, may have worked briefly on the South Western section, but was already in poor condition and was condemned in February 1960; probably having sat at the location seen since the previous year. Note the sandstone mound behind the locomotives: look south from there, and you could view trains entering and leaving Redhill tunnel on the Quarry line, but at a lower level. In the foreground, some Exmouth Junction concrete lamp post components may be seen; perhaps intended to light up the unofficial walkway seen earlier beside the Tonbridge line. Maybe this had now been recognised as an access route to the shed, and the staff had raised the issue of poor lighting during the hours of darkness. Or, maybe, someone had stumbled and received injury, thus prompting some action?   R. Hobbs 1460

Taken from The Mound, near the top of Redstone Hill; looking roughly south-westwards, an unidentified Schools class heads north and is about to enter Redhill Tunnel on the Quarry line, with what may be empty stock destined for the Eastern Region; there are two LNER coaches in the middle of a rake of BR Mk 1 vehicles. The head code indicates Brighton to London Bridge or Bricklayers Arms via Quarry, so perhaps being returned to New Cross Gate or Rotherhithe Road carriage sidings. Above the first coaches, Earlswood substation may be seen, with the line towards Redhill station rising behind. On the left is Earlswood goods yard, with a C2X locomotive engaged in shunting just seen at extreme left, while Earlswood station is out of sight further left, where the Quarry line and that from Redhill station meet up. The goods yard dealt largely with the local coal traffic and is now almost totally occupied by housing development. Redhill shed is out of camera to the right, at a higher level than the Quarry line. The church of St. John the Evangelist, Redhill, dominates the distant skyline. *R. Hobbs 1087*

A slightly more unusual visitor to Redhill; H15 class rebuild No 30331 from Salisbury (72B), in for repairs in January 1960, standing on the wheel drop road. The wheel drop itself was located under the somewhat makeshift-looking corrugated asbestos structure behind. There were 26 examples of class H15 and they were a somewhat mixed bunch. Ten were the original Urie locomotives of 1914 (Nos 482-491), ten more were slightly more modern Maunsell products of 1924 (Nos 473-478 and 521-524), while the other six were rebuilds of Drummond's rather dodgy 4-6-0s. Number 335 began life as the solitary representative of class E14 and was probably Drummond's biggest failure; being rebuilt by Robert Urie as soon as 1914, while numbers 330-334 were Maunsell rebuilds of class F13 dating from 1924; which were not quite as bad, but still a minor nightmare for a footplate crew entrusted with them. No 30331 did re-enter service, as Dick Riley photographed the engine ready to run back to Salisbury on 27 February 1960, but not for long, as withdrawal took place in March 1961. To the left is a former LSWR 56ft four-compartment brake third coach; now serving the shed in departmental use. *R. Hobbs 1586*

This one could not be resisted, and dates from July or August 1964. The writer visited the shed on 31 August and was most surprised to be confronted by 41D Canklow-allocated LNER B1 class 4-6-0 No 61313; in the position seen here. It had arrived on a pigeon special to Lewes on 26 June 1964, proceeding to turn at Eastbourne. There, a hot box was discovered, and it was held at Eastbourne shed until moved to Redhill on 6 July, but not before local enthusiast Sid Nash found and photographed it! Repairs took some time, but once completed the loco worked a van train to Brighton on 30 September 1964 and made two passenger trips to Reading on 1 and 2 October before powering a train of condemned wagons to Streatham Common the following day. It then ran light to Cricklewood and thence returned home. It even acquired a 75B shed plate during its stay, so there might have been some local intention to hang on to the loco! Built by North British Locomotive Company in April 1948, it spent most of its life on the Great Central line but was withdrawn from Langwith Junction shed (41J) in November 1965. On 31 August 1964, Redhill shed was host to locomotives from all four regions as, beside the B1 were two LMS Stanier 8F's and GWR mogul 6309, plus the usual SR moguls and BR standard classes. As a young spotter, one always hoped for the unexpected, but on that day, he was most certainly rewarded. *R. Hobbs 1889*

We now arrive at Redhill station, which had two through lines and three platform lines. On the right, at the down platform (No three) is L class No 31760 on a former SECR Birdcage trio-set, forming the 3.12pm local service to Tonbridge and, by the head code, possibly onwards to Tunbridge Wells West, Eridge, Lewes and Brighton; if so, reaching there by a somewhat circuitous route: it would be far quicker to catch a semi-fast electric train from the same platform direct through Three Bridges and Haywards Heath. It will follow the Bulleid-hauled train out towards Tonbridge. On the far left, at platform one, a BR standard mogul waits with a train to Guildford and Reading, while in platform two original Bullied pacific 34085 *501 Squadron* (then from Ramsgate shed) has coupled up to a Maunsell formation on a late-running inter-regional train to Margate, via Tonbridge and Ashford. The fireman is just affixing the train reporting number 194, so this is a Saturday, and will be the 7.35am from Birkenhead through train that had previously just arrived from the Guildford direction, and whose locomotive is probably still at the London end of the up platform. Departure time from Redhill was scheduled at 2.46pm. The Saturday formation should be 12 coaches, but we can only see the first four, including a Maunsell buffet or cafeteria car. Both platforms one and two could be used for trains arriving and departing to the west, south or east, while platform three could only deal with departures in those directions, not arrivals. However, this picture illustrates the complexities of train working at Redhill; there is no room in the platforms for any electric service between London and Brighton to connect with these trains. The date is not recorded, but probably mid-1957. *R. Hobbs 1004*

Opposite Bottom: Looking south from platform three, a train from Guildford has arrived at platform two in rather snowy conditions, possibly in early 1958, hauled by N class No 31868 and an unidentified BR standard 2-6-4 tank. Clearly, the weather conditions warrant extra power, as the train consists of just a Maunsell three-set and a utility van. Two light engines occupy the through roads, and this was a very common feature of station working here: either that, or a freight train reversing on its journey between Tonbridge and Guildford. Despite the conditions, an electric service may be seen departing southwards, although the through loops might not have seen electric trains that morning. Just seen to the right of the light engines, the line to Reigate and Guildford swings away westwards. Unseen on the left was a north-facing bay line used for parcels traffic; there was (indeed still is) a large regional GPO sorting office adjacent to the station. This continues to function to this day but is no longer rail-served, while the bay road has been out of use since at least the 1980s. *R. Hobbs 1304*

Below: An unidentified C2X 0-6-0 with only a single dome shunts the up yard at Redhill, sometime during 1958 and photographed from what was then the westernmost platform one. The new platform zero now occupies the line where the locomotive is standing, while platform one is now a terminal road: accessed only from the south end with buffers at the north end of the platform, behind the photographer. The yard curves away following the line of the tracks to Reigate and Guildford. The usual selection of wagons is on view, including two BR all-steel minerals, a Continental ferry van, a Southern Conflat D, and a pillbox 25-ton brake van, plus several other vans. Although unseen, the main A25 road passes beneath the station at this point and then rises Redstone Hill on its way eastwards towards Sevenoaks and Wrotham. The Art-Deco Odeon cinema building fronting this road and alongside the station has long gone; it closed as a cinema in 1975 but remained in use as a night-club until 2011 and has now been replaced by a modern apartment block called The Picturehouse. At some point, it was hoped that the facade would be incorporated into the new building, but this was not to be. Indeed, the whole of the immediate station area has been rebuilt, including the station entrance buildings and there is a new roundabout and ring road separating the station from the town itself. But then, the C2X isn't there, either... *R. Hobbs 1030*

On a Saturday in June 1958, L1 class No 31785 departs from island platform one and crosses the entire layout to access the Tonbridge line. Although difficult to see, the route set is shown by an indicator below the signal arm, hence there is just one starter for each platform, whereas the down through line has an arm for each route. In this case, the upper arm signals the line ahead to Earlswood, the lower arm round to Tonbridge. There was no access to the Reigate to Guildford route from the down through line. To access this from the north a train had to use platform three, as did the regular electric services from London to Reigate. The starter on this platform was another single arm, with a route indicator. The loco is on Gillingham duty 245 and had arrived earlier with the 7.17am from Maidstone West with the train reporting number 313. The stock ran through to Reading South, although No 31785 will have come off at Redhill just before 9am. It is now returning eastwards as the 12.07pm Redhill to Tonbridge, although the coaches will continue onwards towards Margate. The train reporting number has remained on the smokebox and will serve to confuse for the rest of the day! The stock is a pair of Maunsell restriction 0 three-sets with No 950 at the front, comprising brake composites 6901/2 and third (now second) 1034, which is how the set ran from 1934 until late 1959. These began their journey as the 10.37am from Reading South, so have not long arrived from the Guildford direction. This proves that the restriction 0 sets were not just confined to Hastings line services. On this occasion at least the station looks relatively quiet. *R. Hobbs 1088*

Bathed in soft evening light, ex-SECR D class 4-4-0 No 31549 waits at the south end of platform three before running light to the shed, sometime during mid-1956. The 51 members of this class were completed between 1901 and 1907; construction being shared between Dubs and Co., Sharp Stewart, Robert Stephenson and Co., Vulcan Foundry and Ashford Works. No 31549 dates from September 1906; one of those built at Ashford and which ran until October 1956; one of the final five in traffic and then based at Guildford shed. They were a Harry Wainwright design; this meant most of the work may be ascribed to Robert Surtees, late of the London, Chatham, and Dover Railway, and so the class incorporated many LCDR details. However, as may be seen, they were aesthetically very pleasing in appearance, and their performance matched that, too. Indeed, the writer's earliest reliably dated memory is the sight of one of these grand old ladies at the buffer stops at Charing Cross, probably in August or September 1956. Twenty-one were rebuilt by Maunsell to class D1 between 1921 and 1927. No 737 remains as part of the National Collection, restored to the magnificent Wainwright SECR livery, and may be viewed today at the NRM in York. *N. Stead 200788*

A picture taken from the footbridge that crosses the northern end of the station throat, perhaps from late 1957. Ex-GWR mogul No 6313 from Reading GWR shed (81D) is waiting to shunt across to the up main, before returning to the station to pick up its train for Reading in either platform one or two. The locomotive has recently been repainted in lined green, complete with new BR emblem; introduced in 1956, but not widely applied until the following year. Despite this, the old Cycling Lion badge used since 1949 could still be seen on locomotives until about 1963. These GWR moguls were regular visitors to Redhill until late 1964, by which time some Manor 4-6-0s and, more occasionally, a Hall, could be seen here. The up and down lines at this point were flanked by a siding and in the up siding may be seen ex-SECR Birdcage trio set 596; withdrawn in January 1958. This comprised brake coaches 3429 and 3501, with composite 5469 in the middle. Built as SECR set 164 in November 1913, it was renumbered as SR set 596 on 7 November 1923 and was one of 72 South Eastern 60ft Trio-C sets built between 1912 and 1921. Loco spotting from this location was nothing like as interesting as from the southern end of the station as, since electrification in 1932, relatively few steam-hauled services left the station northwards and most of these were goods trains. The light-coloured ballast is probably sand, dropped from hopper wagons serving Holmthorpe pits. This is the cue for the next two pictures. *R. Hobbs 1032*

September 1959. A down goods train towards Redhill, hauled by N class mogul No 31867 has reversed into Holmthorpe sidings, near Merstham, with empties for the sand pits, hence the hopper wagon behind the tender. These sidings, once the property of The Standard Brick and Sand Company; later British Industrial Sand, left the down line about two miles north of Redhill station at Holmthorpe signal box, falling away steeply at one in 50 and turning sharply through 90 degrees before passing eastwards under the Quarry line and into the pits themselves. BR locomotives were only allowed as far as the reception sidings, leaving privately-owned small industrial locomotives to shunt the wagons under the Quarry line bridge. Traffic ceased by about 1990, by which time the duty was usually hauled by a Crompton class 33 diesel. SR instructions state that the maximum load to be hauled up the gradient to the main line was eight loaded wagons, often necessitating a second shunt to collect them all. The rather curiously shaped building on the left remains to this day and is easily spotted on Google maps. The site is now partly given over to an industrial estate, partly to housing and partly as a local nature reserve. *R. Hobbs 1441*

Continuing round the curve, we reach the three reception sidings and the limit of BR locomotive operation. In November 1959, C2X No 32451 from Redhill shed has shunted the sidings and is now ready to leave with a full head of steam to attack the one in 50 gradient back up to the main line. The snow is not snow, but sand that has spilled from the wagons. On the left is Trowers Way; now the main thoroughfare through the industrial estate, while behind the Quarry line embankment crosses the site on a north-to-south axis. The railway tracks extend under the bridge seen behind the wagons and into the works proper. In later years, various small diesel locomotives were employed to shunt the wagons, but previously, steam engines were employed. One of these was *Gervase*; a rather odd-looking vertical-boilered 0-4-0 locomotive converted by the Sentinel Locomotive Company in 1928, which worked here from 1949 until acquired by the Kent & East Sussex Railway in 1962. It remained there, largely inactive, until 2008, after which it moved north and was subsequently restored to working order on the Great Central Railway at Loughborough. Since then, it has toured several industrial heritage railways in the Midlands but is now believed to be at The Buckinghamshire Railway Centre at Quainton Road for overhaul. *R. Hobbs 1522*

The view south from platform two looking towards the loco shed; perhaps in about mid-1963 or 1964. New-looking Crompton D6581 is standing in the up through road, while slightly older sister D6568 is signalled away from the down through towards Tonbridge, watched by the crew of BR standard tank 80141 waiting in platform three with a train of Bulleid stock, probably for Tonbridge, as the loco was allocated to Tunbridge Wells West from December 1959 until September 1963. It then moved to Brighton for a very short time before coming to Redhill in January 1964, staying until a final move to Nine Elms in June 1965; one of the last locomotives allocated to Redhill. It was withdrawn from Nine Elms in January 1966. So, this gives a wide date span for the picture. One interesting feature is the stock just visible behind D6568. The coach is a BR Mk 1 in lined maroon, so unlikely to be Southern Region allocated. Just whether it is empty stock, or an inter-regional service cannot be stated from the visible evidence. Also seen is the semi-circular route indicator below the starting signal at the south end of platform two; a feature of all three platform starters at this end of the station. Redhill B signal box may be seen directly ahead. This was a former South Eastern Railway timber-clad structure dating from 1882 but was shrouded in a heavy brick base early in World War Two to protect the locking room from bomb blast. Prior to BR days it was known as Redhill No 2. It closed in May 1985, on the opening of the new Three Bridges signalling centre.
K. Coursey 182

Leaving Redhill for Guildford and Reading and negotiating the sharp curve around towards Reigate, ex-LSWR S11 class 4-4-0 No 30400 hauls a Southern gangwayed bogie luggage van and a Birdcage Trio-C set past the buffer stops of the up yard and the home signals guarding entry into platforms one and two on a rather damp day in 1953. The crew are clearly aware of the photographer's presence. At this time, No 30400 was the sole survivor of the class of ten locomotives and, along with similar sole surviving L12 4-4-0 No 30434, were regular performers from Guildford shed along the line to Reading and Redhill. Both outlasted fellow members of their respective classes by some three years, and both went for scrap between late 1954 and early 1955. Note the calling-on signal arms below the main homes; if one of these was pulled off it indicated that the relevant platform road was already partly occupied. This procedure was regularly employed for the Reigate portion of the electric service to London (usually a 4-LAV unit) to buffer up and couple to another unit that had arrived a little earlier from the Brighton line. The disc signal applied only to shunting moves, usually by a light engine. At that time, it was not possible for trains from the Guildford direction to access the up through line; only into platforms one and two. *N. Stead 200777*

The last route into Redhill came through the Surrey Hills at the foot of the North Downs from Guildford. This was, and remains, the only unelectrified line in the area and is today operated, somewhat incongruously, by First Great Western class 165 and 166 Network Turbo diesel units based at Reading, although these are scheduled for early replacement. Electrification as far as Reigate only took place in mid-1932, and the service was for many years in the hands of 2-BIL or 4-LAV units attached or detached from a Brighton line stopping train at Redhill station. Here, LSWR M7 0-4-4 tank No 30026 hauls a South Eastern Trio-C set towards Redhill, while 4-LAV unit 2937 stands in the down, westbound, platform. The date is not recorded, but tank engines were only occasionally used on the line by the late-1950s. This event could be because one of the turntables at either Reading or Redhill were out of use for repairs. Whatever the explanation, no doubt the cameraman knew of it, and was ready to record the unusual. *R. Hobbs 2296*

Top: Turning and looking in the opposite direction, another tank loco; this time LBSCR E4 No 32515, restarts another Redhill-bound service comprising an LNER four-wheeled brake van and a Maunsell restriction 4 three-set; this is known because a sequence of three pictures was taken. In this one, the loco is nicely framed by the bracket starter signal; mounted to be visible around the station canopy. Again, the date is not recorded but probably August 1958. On this occasion, the electric unit in the other platform was a solitary 2-HAL unit. *R. Hobbs 1037*

Bottom: At the western end of the station, the line crosses the A217 London Road/Reigate Hill on a level crossing, with the typical Southern signal box alongside, dating from 1929. It remains there today, but the crossing is now protected by lifting barriers. For how much longer this situation prevails is not known, as Network Rail plans to reconstruct the station to cater for 12-car electric trains to London. In early 1964 N class mogul No 31862 departs westwards with a train to Guildford and Reading, while an AA Land Rover in yellow and black, followed by a London Transport green-liveried RT from Reigate garage wait at the crossing. The bus will probably be on route 406 from Redhill station to Kingston via Tadworth, Epsom and Tolworth. There were no less than 4825 RT buses, built from 1938 until 1954; including several variants in this total as well as 1631 more with Leyland engines (classified RTL), and 500 others that were six inches wider (classified RTW). They were very much the classic London bus of the 1950s, and the last came out of London service in 1979. In the mist above looms Reigate Hill at a maximum altitude of 771 feet above sea level. The sort of typical 1960s street scene that we took very much for granted. *R. Hobbs 1732*

Schools class No 30909 *St Pauls* about to leave Reigate on a cold morning in December 1958. It shows more typical motive power for a Reading to Redhill train; certainly between 1957 and 1962. The stock is a BR standard Mk 1 three-set (one of 515-571) in crimson lake and cream with a Maunsell 1930/33 open third (now second) in green on the front. The loco carries a 73A Stewart's Lane shed plate but would end its days at Guildford in 1962. This was one of the class equipped with a Lemaitre blast pipe and chimney by Oliver Bulleid between 1939 and 1941. In the background, another Reading-bound train has just departed, and the crossing gates have opened to road traffic. Another green-liveried London Transport RT is crossing the tracks. The down starting signal is, like its counterpart on the up platform, bracketed out to be visible alongside the platform canopy. Electrified tracks end at the level crossing. Regular steam haulage ceased over the line on 3 January 1965, after which the services were in the hands of the 3R Tadpole diesel units numbered 1201-6, plus some Crompton-hauled corridor trains during rush hours. *R. Hobbs 1299*

We finally leave the Redhill area with Bulleid West Country pacific 34046 *Braunton* coming down from Redhill station and approaching Earlswood, where the Quarry line comes in on the right immediately behind the locomotive. The date is probably 1958; the train has originated on the London Midland Region and reached Southern metals over the West London line and through Kensington Olympia. *Braunton* was then one of the relatively few Brighton-based pacifics and on her way home. She was allocated there from 1951, until withdrawn for rebuilding in January 1961 She's recorded as being the last member of the class to receive attention at Brighton Works before they closed in April 1958. After rebuilding, the loco went to the SW section until finally taken out of traffic in October 1965. However, this was not the end, and the locomotive was subsequently purchased for preservation and has done two sessions of main line running, commencing in 2013 and still going at the time of writing. The rather mixed Maunsell eight-set included both restriction 1 and restriction 4 stock, while the first digit of the set number is 4, giving several possibilities. The train is signalled to continue along the local line towards Three Bridges instead of crossing to the fast line at this point. Perhaps engineering works are in progress on the Quarry line and this is the reason that the train has come through Redhill? *R. Hobbs 1007*

The last ex-LBSCR D3 0-4-4 tank was No 32390; seen here ready to leave Three Bridges station before working the RCTS East Sussex Rail Tour on 4 October 1953. This visited East Grinstead, Eridge, the Cuckoo line to Polegate (reverse), Lewes, including the goods yard lines and then back to Three Bridges, again via East Grinstead, where it traversed the goods connecting line between the low- and high-level stations. The stock was ex-LBSCR pull-push set 727 in lined crimson lake livery. Note that although both locomotive and stock are PP-equipped, most, if not all, the tour was not operated in pull-push mode, as the loco is coupled at the driving end of the set. The D3 class was introduced by R. J. Billinton in 1892, and 36 were built between then and 1896. Billinton had come from the Midland Railway at Derby, where similar 0-4-4 tanks had been built, so this was likely to be the origin of the design. The first locomotive of the class, LBSCR No 363, carried the name Goldsmid after the then Chairman of the company; Sir Julian Goldsmid, and an image of the engine was soon incorporated into LBSCR staff cap badges. Two were rebuilt by Marsh into class D3X in the same manner as the C2X, E4X, etc., but this did not result in any advantage (it certainly did not improve their appearance!) and so the rest of the class remained substantially as built. Withdrawals commenced in 1933, and by the date of this picture, No 32390 alone remained in traffic, until September 1955. Three Bridges station was somewhat similar geographically to Redhill, with the Brighton main line running north-to-south, the Horsham and mid-Sussex line turning off sharply westwards, and the branch to East Grinstead and Tunbridge Wells turning off eastwards. Another picture of this tour appears later at Polegate. *K. Coursey 358*

Passengers arriving at East Grinstead today, perhaps visiting the Bluebell Railway, would not recognise this view of East Grinstead station. This was the four-platform high-level station running on a roughly east-to-west axis and serving trains between Tunbridge Wells West and Three Bridges as well as those towards Oxted and London. None of this remains today. On 4 April 1959, H class tank No 31269 is about to shunt forward and reverse into the platform on the right (the shunt signal is off for the move), watched by a youthful enthusiast before leaving slightly later for Three Bridges hauling a pull-push set; probably after connection has been made with an Oxted line train. The station can be seen to have two island platforms and if one looks carefully, the bridge parapets over the north-to-south axis low-level station may be seen to the right of the running-in board and to the left of the observer. The entrances to the stairways connecting these platforms and the low-level station may also be seen beneath the canopies. *A. E. Bennett 4607*

Looking in the other direction on the same day, another H class, No 31329, departs on the single line towards Three Bridges propelling a pull-push set and watched by the same observer. The train is just passing the west signal box, while on the right, the sharply curved and graded double track spur towards St. Margaret's Junction caters for trains to and from Oxted and London. The platform from which the train is leaving only serves the Three Bridges line; the other three could all be accessed by trains to or from Oxted. The history of East Grinstead and its stations is complicated: the one seen is the third provided for the town. The original station dates from the arrival of the line from Three Bridges in 1855 and was slightly nearer the town centre than all later stations. When this line was extended eastwards towards Tunbridge Wells a new station was built slightly further west than the original, opening in 1866. The arrival of both the Lewes and East Grinstead Railway (from the south) and the Croydon, Oxted and East Grinstead Railway (from the north) required new platforms on a north-to-south axis, and to accommodate these, the entire station was rebuilt between 1882 and 1883 into a six-platform interchange; with four east-west high level and two north-south low-level platforms; giving a cross-shaped station if viewed from the air. Two connecting spurs were provided; a goods yard link from south to east and St Margaret's spur from the north around to just west of the high-level platforms, thereby completing the layout that would remain in place until 1970. Closure of the Three Bridges to Tunbridge Wells line took place in January 1967, thereby rendering the high-level station redundant from that date and this was demolished between 1970 and 1971; trains having then returned to the low-level platforms. A new pre-cast Clasp station building situated adjacent to the lower-level platforms was then provided, and this served until a further rebuilding between 2012 and 2013; when the Bluebell Railway recommenced services into their own station from Horsted Keynes and Sheffield Park. *A. E. Bennett 4606*

We are now on East Grinstead's lower platforms. These might just about be recognised by modern travellers, although none of the buildings seen here remain today. These platforms became redundant in 1955 on closure of the line southwards towards Horsted Keynes and Lewes, but, thanks to the more recent success of the Bluebell Railway, the subsequent history of this line is now well-known to enthusiasts. Residents unearthed a clause in the original Lewes & East Grinstead Railway Act that required the railway to provide the service for 999 years unless prior legal notice had been given. BR had failed to do this and were thus obliged to reinstate a minimal service, which took place from 7 August 1956. On this day C2X No 32442 has charge of LBSCR two-coach pull-push set 504 (the other one that was intended for Isle of Wight transfer in 1938 along with set 503 but never sent there), on one of the first services to Lewes since 28 May 1955; the novelty being watched by several residents. The low-level platforms have clearly been fettled up for the reinstatement. BR had no intention of long-term provision and took immediate legal steps to repeal the original L and EGR Act, enabling them to successfully close the line for the second time on 17 March 1958. During this period, there was a service of just four trains per day; usually just a single coach and using whatever motive power could be mustered for the trains. It was not advertised in any way and became known to the locals as "the sulky service". Of course, nobody realised then what the future held for the line once the preservationists took charge! The high-level platforms may be seen in the background, with an ex-LSWR corridor pull-push set on a Tunbridge Wells West to Three Bridges working. *A. E. Bennett 1537A*

We now move on to Tunbridge Wells West; the LBSCR's most imposing terminal station of 1866. It became a through station soon after, when a spur was constructed through to the South Eastern's Tonbridge-Hastings line at Grove Junction. However, relatively few trains used this connecting line, and most Central section services would continue to terminate here from a westerly direction. On 16 March 1957, C class goods No 31223 leaves platform three with unique BR standard Mk 1 non-corridor set 904. This set (originally of just three coaches) was intended to become Exmouth branch set 156, along with similar sets 152-155, but was diverted to the Oxted line before it arrived at Exeter, together with two non-corridor third coaches to form commuter-set 904 to overcome crowding on several morning and evening rush-hour trains to and from London. An additional composite coach was required, but no matching BR vehicle was available, so ex-LSWR rebuilt 58ft lavatory composite S4727S was used instead, the fourth coach in the train. The other vehicles were brake third S43382, third S46297, composite S41064, then the LSWR coach, third S46298 and brake third S43383. This ran so formed, in crimson lake livery, from 1956 until October 1958, when two green Bulleid corridor composites replaced the LSWR vehicle. After June 1956, all third-class compartments were, or course, relabelled second class. Later, two BR corridor composites were used, but the set continued to run on the Oxted line until 1965. The head code displayed is for the Cuckoo line to Eastbourne, but this is not relevant as the loco is just moving the empty stock to a siding. In the far distance, an ex-LBSCR pull-push set occupies bay platform two while D1 No 31492 stands in platform five, having previously brought set 904 down from London Bridge via Hever. The rather austere goods shed contrasts with the magnificent station building. The station closed in 1985 and the station building now serves as a wild west-themed restaurant. The locomotive shed is just visible on the left (coded 75F in BR days) and is now the headquarters and workshop of the Spa Valley Railway. Most of the rest of the station area is now a supermarket and its car park. *R. C. Riley 8124*

We are now standing on platform three at Tunbridge Wells West, sometime in 1958. L class 4-4-0 No 31777 is at platform four on a train from Tonbridge to Brighton, having just traversed the single-line connection from the Tonbridge-Hastings route, and arrived from the eastern end of the station. On leaving Groombridge, the train will take the southern fork of the junction towards Eridge, Uckfield and Lewes. The stock is a Maunsell restriction 0 three-set, almost certainly No 476 comprising brake composites 6887/88 and corridor third 1026, with an unidentified SECR Continental third on the rear. In platform five, Fairburn LMR tank No 42068 waits to follow with a train to Victoria via Hever and Oxted, formed of Bulleid/BRCW three-set 800. This will turn northwards after Groombridge, and head towards Oxted. The Fairburn was one of 41 examples (Nos 42066-106) built at Brighton Works between 1950 and 1951 for the Southern Region and used to replace many obsolete pre-Grouping Southern types. The sort of locomotive that Bulleid ought to have built for the company instead of developing his Leader class! A few did not stay long but most remained until 1959, then being swapped for an equivalent number of BR standard 2-6-4 tanks. In bay platform one (on the left) is a BR Mk 1 corridor three-set while in the far distance a U1 class Mogul stands in bay platform two at the head of other stock. Tunbridge Wells West was once a busy station, and the hub of Central section services east of the London-Brighton main line, and it is perhaps surprising that usage declined so much that it closed in July 1985. Indeed, in its heyday in 1955, no less than 136 trains called on a normal weekday, serving no less than six different routes. Although the station building was grade two listed in 1986 and survives, none of the platform infrastructure now exists and the present-day Spa Valley Railway operates from a small new station alongside the locomotive shed. *N. Stead 200977*

On shed at Tunbridge Wells West on 4 February 1950 is ex-LBSCR J2 class 4-6-2 tank No 32326; originally named *Bessborough* after Lord Bessborough, once Chairman of the company. Two of these impressive tanks were completed at Brighton in 1910 and 1912, the other was J1 No 32325, once named *Abergavenny,* and both spent much of the post-war period based at Tunbridge Wells until September 1950. No 32326 differed in having Walschaerts valve gear instead of Stephenson's and was considered the better engine of the two. Still carrying Southern Railway lined malachite green livery, albeit now lettered British Railways and not so clean, the two locos could be seen on services to London, Brighton, Eastbourne and occasionally to Redhill, and were amongst the classes replaced by the Fairburn tanks seen in the previous picture. For their final months, both were transferred to Brighton where they were used on a variety of duties, until withdrawn in June 1951. The four-road shed was home to many ex-LBSCR tank classes over the years, but as the 1950s progressed, these gave way to more modern LMR and BR standard classes until closure in June 1965, however the building continued to house Engineer's stock until the late 1970s, which enabled it to survive to be taken over by the Spa Valley Railway. *L. R. Freeman F219*

Looking eastwards on a crisp 17 March 1962, this is Groombridge, viewed from the road bridge just west of the station. BR Standard 2-6-4 tank No 80032 blasts out of the station for Brighton, timed at 11.50am. One can almost hear the bark of the exhaust from the picture! New from Brighton Works in March 1952, the loco was allocated just across the road at 75A, so is heading for home. A move to Redhill took place in January 1964, with one more move to Bournemouth in June 1965. Withdrawal occurred from there in January 1967. The stock is Maunsell restriction 1 four-set No 189. By this date, many Oxted line services were in the hands of the Standard tanks and indeed, just two minutes later No 80139 was photographed coming in the opposite direction. The main station building is on the down platform, towards Tunbridge Wells West, and the up side comprises an island platform for trains going towards Uckfield, East Grinstead or direct towards Oxted and London through Hever; allowing some form of cross-platform interchange when required. The substantial goods shed may be seen behind the bracket-mounted starting signal. Beyond the station, the Groombridge triangle also allowed direct running from Ashurst towards Eridge; a route used by some steam-hauled London-Brighton via Oxted services. It was a whole network of lines that have, today, almost been decimated and now just the class 171 diesel-hauled service to Uckfield remains. The case for electrification has often been put forward, but like reinstatement of the line to Lewes beyond Uckfield, little real progress has been made and several obstacles now lie in the route of that line. *J. Harrold 3510*

The RCTS East Sussex Rail Tour of 4 October 1953 has now reached Polegate over the Cuckoo line and Hailsham, where reversal towards Lewes took place. D3 No 32390 has uncoupled from the pull-push set and proceeded to the eastern end of the platform to take water; watched and photographed by the enthusiasts. The locomotive will then run round before coupling up to the correct end of set 727 before setting off eastwards for Lewes; the ringed signal arm allowing entry to the goods sidings and run-round loop already being pulled off. An impressive array of Southern Railway upper-quadrant signals may be seen, controlling the line straight ahead towards Stone Cross, Bexhill and Hastings and sharp right towards Eastbourne. Many passenger services would take the latter route and only goods trains and a few inter-regionals would traverse the northern side of the triangle. Today, this section has been lifted and all trains must go via Eastbourne. From time to time, the residents of Bexhill and Hastings have requested that this side of the triangle is reinstated to obviate the reversal through Eastbourne, but this has come to nothing. Polegate station has also moved: back to its original site. The original station opened with the line to Hastings in 1846 but sometime after the Hailsham branch opened the station was re-sited some 440 yards further east to facilitate easier interchange between trains to Hailsham, Eastbourne and Hastings. The Hailsham branch closed in 1968, and in 1986 a new station was built on the original 1846 site, which had always been more convenient for the town. The old station became a public house and restaurant. It was demolished in 2017, but not before a complete archaeological survey of the building was made by SWAT Archaeology Limited. *K. Coursey 357*

Eastbourne station, sometime during the mid-1950s. Semi-fast 2-NOL (NO-Lavatories) electric unit 1820 waits to leave from platform two for Brighton, while a 6-PAN unit stands in platform three. Just visible on the right is a BR standard three-set on a train for Tunbridge Wells West, headed by Fairburn tank 42102 (there is another picture in the sequence). There were 78 of these two-car electric units, built between 1934 and 1936; they were a common sight at Eastbourne from 1935 until final withdrawal in 1959. The timber bodywork came from ex-LSWR steam stock, on new 62ft underframes. Unit 1820 comprised motor brake third 9868 and driving trailer composite 9947, running from December 1934 until July 1959. These were some of the last timber-bodied electric units to run on the Southern Region and their demise was hastened after the Barnes rear-end collision of December 1955, when electric arcing set fire to similar unit 1853 resulting in 13 deaths. As a result, withdrawal of all timber-bodied coaches; not just electric stock but any remaining steam-hauled vehicles, was accelerated. The impressive architecture of the station may be seen above the coaches: restored to full glory during a major refurbishment that is still ongoing, and now includes a matching covered pedestrian and road vehicle canopy over the area once occupied by platform four. *K. Coursey 481*

At Eastbourne shed in 1948, we see LBSCR I3 class 4-4-2 tank No 32090, shortly after being repainted in BR livery: with the number in SR-style transfers but with hand-painted plain British Railways lettering on the tanks. Unlike many of Douglas Earle Marsh's locomotives, the I3s were an instant success and, once superheated, proved efficient and economical machines. A total of 27 were completed between 1907 and 1913. Apart from No 2024, withdrawn in 1944, all the rest lasted until between 1950 and 1952. Those at Eastbourne in the late 1940s were used mostly over the Cuckoo line to Tunbridge Wells West or on inter-regional trains between Hastings and Brighton. Like the J1 and J2 pacific tanks, their days were numbered once the Fairburn 2-6-4 tanks were available. For No 32090, the end came in November 1950. Eastbourne shed became synonymous with condemned and stored engines during and after World War Two; electrification to the town took place in 1935, so the shed was large, modern but under-utilised. It was damaged during wartime bombing raids, but continued to function until June 1965, when steam-haulage over the line to Tunbridge Wells came to an end. *N. Stead 200880A*

Heading a rather mixed formation on a Brighton-Tonbridge service is large radial E5 class tank No 2573; still carrying full Southern livery at Lewes on 7 August 1950. One of the 30 examples of Billinton radials with 5ft 6in driving wheels, this ran from February 1903 to July 1953 and originally carried the name *Nutbourne*. It may never have received its full BR livery but despite the lack of attention from the painters, clearly has a good head of steam for the journey out across the rooftops of Lewes town towards Uckfield and Tunbridge Wells. The train comprises a gangwayed bogie luggage van, a Maunsell corridor third still in Southern malachite, a Bulleid corridor composite in crimson lake and cream, with a SECR Birdcage three-set on the rear. The SR operating authorities were seldom concerned if stock matched; either in livery or in appearance, the important matter was to get the right number and proportions of first- and third-class seats in the train. Those of us who model and like tidy and uniform train formations, please note! Lewes station is another that had a complicated history, and a complicated track layout as well. Here, we are viewing the four platforms looking towards Brighton: the three London platforms curve around to the right. *R. C. Riley 4103*

Turning and looking in the other direction a year later, on 4 July 1951, H2 class Atlantic No 32426 *St Alban's Head* arrives from the Uckfield direction and crosses the junctions to gain the Brighton line platforms. The train has originated from London Bridge and run via Oxted, East Grinstead and Sheffield Park and is formed of a 50ft/54ft SECR Birdcage Trio-A set in lined crimson lake livery. From the shadows, the time is evening, so this is probably the 4.20pm departure from London Bridge, due at Lewes at 6.37pm. It would have set out with six coaches; the other three for Tonbridge, and these would have been detached at East Croydon, probably being taken onwards four minutes later by a tank loco from Tunbridge Wells West shed. By the early 1950s, the five surviving Brighton Atlantics did not have any regularly rostered duties, but were used by Brighton shed to cover failures, special workings, and relief Newhaven boat trains. As such, they could turn up in odd places but possibly the strangest was 32421 in April 1953, when it twice managed to reach Yeovil Town on a stopping train from Salisbury; probably the farthest west that a Brighton tender locomotive ever travelled. And for anybody wondering about geography, St Alban's (or St Aldhelm's) Head is just south-west of Swanage, on the Isle of Purbeck. *R. C. Riley 4267*

Focus on Brighton

The station at Brighton opened in May 1840 for services westwards along the coast to Shoreham; the line from London not reaching there until September 1841. The LBSCR established their locomotive works adjacent to the station soon after. This became very much the focus of the company for the remainder of its independent existence, thereby ensuring that the town developed rapidly to become the thriving centre that is today. The carriage and wagon works removed to Lancing in 1909 but, apart from a period in the 1930s, locomotive construction and repair continued until 1958. Electrification of the main line took place from 1 January 1933, and this reduced the number of steam locomotives to be seen, but as the following pictures will show, there was still plenty for the enthusiast to enjoy right up to the 1960s.

Many special trains were run to Brighton Works for the benefit of enthusiasts. Here, on 23 June 1956, we see a Stephenson Locomotive Society special ready to return to London Bridge behind K class mogul No 32337, suitably bulled-up for the occasion. The time is near 6.30pm and the return run was made via Steyning, Horsham and Epsom, unlike the outward journey which came direct via the Quarry line behind N15X class 4-6-0 No 32329 Stephenson. The 17 members of class K were, in the opinion of many, the best of all the Brighton engines and, had Grouping not taken place there might have been at least three more of the class. However, once Maunsell and the Ashford team took over, it was inevitable that they preferred their own N class mogul design, and the outstanding order was cancelled. All 17 remained allocated to Central section sheds and No 32337 was no exception: here seen carrying a 70F (Fratton) shed plate. They might reach as far east as Ashford, often for overhaul, or westwards to Eastleigh for the same reason, and more occasionally to Bournemouth or Salisbury. No 32337 was the prototype and dates from September 1913, although No 32353, the final member of the class, did not take to the rails until March 1921. However, all were condemned at the stroke of an accountant's pen in November and December 1962; not because they were worn out, but to satisfy the Southern Region's quota of withdrawals for the period. The photographer's shutter has not quite frozen the movement of the electric unit departing alongside. *A. E. Bennett 1304*

As noted in the last caption, the SLS special reached Brighton earlier on the same day behind N15X No 32329 *Stephenson;* here is the locomotive at Brighton shed after being turned to be made ready to return to its home shed 70D Basingstoke; where all seven members of the class had by then congregated. Brighton station may be seen in the background, while the assembled enthusiasts record the immaculate loco surrounded by all the detritus of a working engine shed. All seven engines were built as Baltic 4-6-4 class L tanks, emerging from Brighton Works between 1914 (two) and 1922 (five), for the company's principal express services. Trouble was experienced with poor riding of the first two locos, shades of what would be found with Maunsell's River tanks, but after some redesign and modification; complete success was achieved. All seven gave good service between London and Brighton until electrification in 1933, after which they were transferred to Eastbourne. Electrification caught up with them again in 1935, and the decision was taken to rebuild them into 4-6-0 tender locomotives for service on the South Western section. No 2329 was the first rebuild; dealt with at Eastleigh Works between July and December 1934, and then coupled with an eight-wheeled tender taken from S15 No 833, which in turn received a six-wheeled tender as replacement. The other six Baltics were dealt with similarly by April 1936. They were then allocated to Nine Elms and rostered for similar duties to that depot's Lord Nelson and King Arthur 4-6-0s but were soon found wanting in such a capacity. However, all was not lost and after several minor modifications the class settled down into secondary passenger service, which is how they came to be concentrated at Basingstoke shed by 1947. Withdrawals began in 1955, but No 32329 lasted until July 1956; just long enough to provide the SLS motive power on the day photographed, and to power another special a fortnight later. No 32331 survived for one further year. No 32329 returned to Brighton on 12 July 1956, still looking immaculate; but for breaking up. *A. E. Bennett 1292C*

As an additional part of the SLS tour on 23 June 1956, participants could take a round trip to Kemp Town, but had to fork out an additional 2/6d (12 and a half pence in today's money) for the privilege! This might seem like a trifling amount to us, but clearly not everyone was keen, and a two-coach pull-push unit (No 650) sufficed for those who paid the extra fare. Motive power was provided by A1X Terrier tank No 377S, normally the Brighton Works shunter, and not often seen elsewhere. Here, the train is ready to return to Brighton from Kemp Town terminus, which then operated as a goods depot serving the eastern side of the Brighton conurbation. No 377S was built as a class A1 in 1878, LBSCR No 35 and named Morden. It was placed on the duplicate list in November 1908 and renumbered 635, rebuilt to class A1X in April 1922, and became SR No 2635 after 1931. In 1946, the Southern decided to restore former Brighton Works shunter and sister-engine 380S to its original LBSCR condition as No 82 Boxhill, including Stroudley livery for exhibition purposes. It had a stock of this paint left over, so the replacement Brighton Works shunter, No 2635, was specially finished in this livery and renumbered 377S for the purpose. The locomotive retained the livery for the rest of its life; even when restored to capital stock and renumbered to 32635 in January 1959. As such, it acquired something of a celebrity status, and was requested to work several special trains during the period that it carried the livery; including the one illustrated here. The colour was officially referred to as improved engine green: improved, quite possibly, but green; definitely not! More of a mustard yellow colour, which some people described as gamboge. The dictionary definition of this is a gum resin used as a yellow pigment. Withdrawal came in March 1963, but unlike most of the other 1963 Terrier withdrawals this loco did not make it into preservation; being cut up at Eastleigh Works instead. *A. E. Bennett 1300A*

On a different occasion, 13 April 1958, restored LSWR T3 No 563 stands outside Brighton shed: this time on the day of the RCTS Sussex Coast Limited enthusiasts' special to Newhaven and Brighton. This was the final duty for the last Brighton Atlantic; No 32424 *Beachy Head*. The T3 was the last surviving Adams 4-4-0 and had been restored to LSWR livery for the 1948 centenary of Waterloo station, where it was exhibited with Terrier No 82 *Boxhill* (just seen left). The loco has been shunted out by the diesel seen behind and is in the company of another LSWR loco; an M7 0-4-4 tank. After the Waterloo exhibition closed, the two engines were stored in Farnham carriage sheds and other locations. They appeared from time to time at various events but were eventually found a permanent home in the Museum of British Transport at Clapham in 1961. This was not permanent, and in 1973 both engines went to the National Railway Museum at York. From there, No 563 was gifted to the Swanage Railway in 2017 and is currently being restored at the Flour Mill workshops of the Forest of Dean Railway for eventual use at Swanage; hopefully with a return to steam during 2023. *A. Swain D18-1*

Returning to 23 April 1956, our intrepid photographer Tony has walked along Terminus Road, and up the hill outside Brighton station to capture the view looking north from Howard Place. The locomotive shed is visible, as is the main line towards Preston Park, and the coast line turning east across London Road viaduct. The works buildings may also be seen on the right, with Brighton signal box adjacent, just outside the station which is out of view to the lower right. Locomotives seen include a P class 0-6-0T, K class 32339, BR standard tank 80017, West Country pacific 34044 *Woolacombe*, a King Arthur, together with two M7s, two radial tanks, C2Xs, moguls, Atlantics and a Fairburn 2-6-4 tank. The enormous water tank and the water softening plant appear in the centre of the photograph. The coast line westwards, served by platforms one and two in the station may just be seen at the bottom of the picture. Of course, the railway scene looks rather different today! *A. E. Bennett 1291A*

From time to time, usually when Eastleigh was inundated with work, Brighton would undertake overhauls of ex-LSWR locomotives. Here is a broadside view of smart-looking Adams G6 0-6-0T No 30266 alongside the water treatment plant, almost certainly after its final overhaul, sometime between 1951 and 1956; but probably nearer 1951 than later. There were 34 examples of the class, built at Nine Elms Works between 1894 and 1900, so some were completed under Drummond's superintendency, and they varied somewhat in details. There were at least two (possibly as many as five) types of boiler fitted, together with at least two types of smokeboxes, although the overall dimensions of the two fittings combined did not vary by much. Also, where longer boilers were provided, then these engines had a slightly longer coupled wheelbase to accommodate the firebox between the rear pair of axles. It is all rather more complicated than previous texts would imply, so modellers beware! Only 12 received BR livery and numbers after 1948; most of the others were condemned between 1948 and 1951 still carrying Southern lettering, after which there was a lull until 1958. No 30266 lasted at Salisbury shed until late 1959. The final survivor was No 30238, which as departmental No DS682 had served at Meldon Quarry between 1960 and 1962. It replaced former classmate 30272 which, numbered as DS3152, had performed the same function from 1950 to 1960. *K. Coursey 603*

Probably photographed on the same day, ex-SECR E1 class 4-4-0 No 31507 stands in Brighton shed yard. It carries a 73B Bricklayers Arms shed plate, so has possibly arrived on a train from either Tunbridge Wells via Uckfield, or down the main line from Redhill. Harry Wainwright's E class 4-4-0s were an enlargement of his D class, and 26 were built at Ashford Works between 1906 and 1908. Richard Maunsell and his team applied the same D1 class rebuilding treatment to 11 members of the E class between 1919 and 1920, with the same excellent results and the rebuilds were then almost indistinguishable from the D1 class. Telling a D1 from an E1 was always difficult; the writer's method was to look at the coupling rods: on a D1 they were flush, on an E1 they were fluted. It usually seemed to work! Note that the tender is blank, without the British Railways lettering or cycling lion emblem, indicative of a repaint of about 1949 or so. No 31507 was one of three members of the class to be transferred to Nine Elms on completion of phase one of the Kent Coast electrification in June 1959, but they did not stay there long and were soon sent to Salisbury as replacements for withdrawn LSWR T9s. Crews there did not appreciate them, and No 31507 was soon back at Bricklayers Arms, from where withdrawal took place in July 1961. *K. Coursey 604*

Another H2 Atlantic, No 32422 *North Foreland* leaving Brighton shed yard, probably on the same day. The head code discs indicate the through train to Southampton and Bournemouth West, a regular duty for the class. The date is not recorded, but sometime after March 1951 when British Railways lined black livery was applied. This engine ran until failing with a blown out left cylinder cover at East Croydon in August 1956, although it had latterly been restricted to lighter duties owing to a suspected bogie frame flaw. This was discovered a few months earlier, when LNER 4-6-4 No 60700 had been derailed through a similar fault; both types shared the same design of leading bogie. Again, for those interested in geography, North Foreland is in Thanet; between Margate and Broadstairs. *K. Coursey 600*

One of the LMS Fairburn-designed 2-6-4 tanks built at Brighton between 1950 and 1951 for the Southern Region service; No 42093 stands in Brighton shed yard, no exact date but probably mid-late 1951. Sister-engine 42102 is just seen beyond. By 1950, the Southern still had many pre-Grouping small tank locomotives on its books; like the LBSCR I1X, I3, D1, D3s, the LSWR M7 and T1 classes, plus some 4-4-0 tender locos that were well past their prime and in need of urgent replacement. The traffic department had long requested suitable replacements, but perhaps Bulleid was more interested in exploring the technical possibilities of his Leader class rather than designing workaday medium-sized tank engines. Between April and June 1948, the Southern had temporary loan of two members of the class; Nos 42198/99 and these ran a few trials based at both Nine Elms and Tunbridge Wells West. These must have proven successful, as Brighton Works undertook construction of the final 41 of these 2-6-4 tanks and Crewe built 30 of the smaller Ivatt class 2 tanks expressly for SR use. Both classes must have been a Godsend to the hard-pressed motive power department. The Fairburns were allocated mostly to the Central and Eastern sections, although four, including No 42102, did migrate as far as Exmouth Junction for a short time during late 1951 and early 1952. *K. Coursey 602*

Following on from the Fairburn tanks, the new BR CME, Robert Riddles, developed the design further, and from 1951 the BR standard version began to appear from Brighton. A total of 130 of the 155 examples were completed there; with the last, No 80154 being turned out in March 1957; the final engine to be built at the works and then allocated to Brighton shed. No 80014 seen here, the fifth engine of the class to be completed stands in company with an ex-SECR C class and, behind it, E class No 31273 on a unrecorded date in 1951. Without its 75F (Tunbridge Wells West) shed plate, the locomotive could be brand new. These locomotives proved extremely competent, and, unlike earlier SR 2-6-4 tanks, there was no hint of unsteady riding at speed. One wonders why; technology had moved on and track ballasting had been much improved, but maybe the change of civil engineer in 1944 on the retirement of George Ellson had removed the major obstacle to such designs being used over Southern metals. Perhaps, with unfortunate timing, Ellson had taken up the CCE's post just weeks before the Sevenoaks derailment, and this coloured his judgement forever on the matter. Certainly, relations between the Southern's CME and the CCE were never the same after that event. No 80014 moved to Brighton shed in 1963 and was withdrawn from Eastleigh in June 1964. Not a long working life by any means, but not the shortest of the class; that honour falling to No 80103 which managed less than seven and a half years in traffic. K. Coursey 599B

Returning to Brighton station, we see the last working Stroudley D1 class 0-4-2 tank, No 2252, departing from platform three for Horsham during the Summer of 1950, hauling LBSCR pull-push set 719. The latter has already received BR lined crimson lake livery, but the D1 would not be repainted before withdrawal in September 1950. Built as long ago as January 1882, it was LBSCR No 252 and was named *Buckhurst*. Then allocated to Horsham shed, its final duties took the loco to either Guildford via Cranleigh or Brighton via Steyning. Apart from removal of condensing pipes, the blanking plates may be seen on the tank front and the smokebox, and the acquisition of a Drummond chimney, it is still substantially as built. Sister-engine 2253 lasted almost as long, in service from Tunbridge Wells West shed until late 1949. Two others were destined to remain in stock for longer, but semi-derelict. Departmental No 701S (formerly No 2284) and No 2359 remained on the books until 1951, but neither turned a wheel during their final couple of years. In contrast, some members of the class had been withdrawn as long ago as 1903! In platform two is E5X 0-6-2 tank No 32576; one of the E5s rebuilt with a C2X boiler and is waiting to remove empty stock to Hove sidings. A 4-LAV electric unit stands in the front portion of platform three. N. Stead 200881

Moving inside the station; the same service some eleven years later in 1961. Ivatt 2 2-6-2 tank No 41301 waits to leave platform two for Horsham. The stock is a Maunsell pull-push set and a SECR pull-push equipped long ten 60ft second, but motor train operation had almost ceased at Brighton by this time. Both the Brighton-Horsham and Horsham-Guildford services were now in the capable hands of the LMS Ivatt 2 tanks, and another is at the buffer stops, having brought the stock in on an earlier arrival from Horsham. Thirty of the class (No 41290-41319) had been built at Crewe Works especially for the Southern Region between 1951 and 1952. In time, almost half of the class found their way onto the region and could be seen anywhere from Ramsgate in the east to Padstow in the west. Wherever they went, they were almost invariably welcomed and were ideal modern replacements for the smaller pre-Grouping tank classes. A few lasted to the final day of steam on 9 July 1967. They were another class to have a subsidiary Southern Region power classification added; to most they were just power class two, but some of those allocated to the Southern were marked 2P2FA over the running number. In platform three is a 2-HAL unit on a shuttle service to West Worthing. Platform three was unique in that departures could head westwards, London-bound, or eastwards towards Lewes. *N. Stead 200961*

We now return to Three Bridges up the LBSCR main line. The locomotive shed here was a three-road structure situated in the fork of the lines south to Brighton and west towards Horsham. In fact, the second shed at this exact location, it was at least the third to be sited in the vicinity of the station since the Horsham branch opened in 1848. This shed dates from 1909 and housed a range of ex-LBSCR types until the 1950s, when BR standard and Ivatt tanks started to take over. For many years it operated with nearby Horsham shed until the 1930s, but with its central position and the growth of the adjacent marshalling yard gained complete independence, with a maximum allocation of 33 engines in 1933. Once electrification of the main line took place in 1932, the depot allocation started to reduce. Eventually the tables were turned, and Horsham became a sub-shed of Three Bridges. Closure came in January 1964, but locomotives for the Horsham-Guildford and Horsham-Brighton services were stabled here for a year or so afterwards, including diesels until April 1969. The turntable was situated on the right, near the engine hoist. The building was then used for wagon repairs until demolition sometime in the 1970s. Here, in 1961 a selection of locos may be seen, including a 350hp (later class 08) diesel shunter, SR mogul, K, C2X, H, E4 and, possibly a Q class. More recently, a new Thameslink depot has opened on part of the extensive goods and permanent way yard site, so there is still a maintenance capability at Three Bridges. *N. Stead 200962S*

Opened in 1896, Horsham shed was located at the London end of the station, adjacent to the junction of the lines to Dorking and Three Bridges. Unusually, it was an 18-road semi-roundhouse situated around a turntable, and only eight miles from Three Bridges, so for many years both sheds operated pretty much as one. Some sources say that it became a sub-shed of Three Bridges in 1959, but here is Q class No 30544 alongside the turntable on 16 April 1961, still carrying a 75D Horsham shed plate. The roundhouse building is visible to the right. The allocation was mostly ex-LBSCR tanks and a few 0-6-0s for local goods work, plus the odd K class, while from about 1949 several LSWR M7 tanks appeared. At the end, in 1964, several of the Ivatt 2 2-6-2 tanks could be found here for the Guildford and Brighton line services. The Qs were Maunsell's last steam class and were designed just prior to his retirement during a period of ill-health, so it may be that not so much thought went into their design. They did not actually enter service until after his retirement. Opinion has varied regarding their effectiveness (or mediocrity!) and a certain amount of modification was made after construction was completed; including the provision by Bulleid of multi-jet blast pipes and chimneys, as seen here. However, this did not appear to give very much improvement, while No 30549 was equipped in 1955 with a BR Standard 4 blast pipe coupled with a rather ugly stove pipe chimney: giving the loco the nickname of the spout. Surprisingly, this improved the steaming, and the appearance was much improved later by the fitting of a Standard 4 chimney. Six other members of the class were similarly equipped between 1958 and 1961 but the rest, including No 30544 were left unaltered. Withdrawn for this engine came in January 1964. It is interesting to note that the Bluebell Railway have provided a BR blast pipe and chimney on No 30541; a fitting that this loco did not have in BR ownership, and in this condition, it has proved a worthwhile addition to their stud. *N. Nicholson 2119*

Horsham station was reconstructed by the Southern Railway in Art Deco form ready for the extension of the mid-Sussex line electrification in 1938 and is now grade two listed. It then provided two island platforms as seen here and it was the terminating point for suburban electric services through Leatherhead and Dorking. Apart from Summer Sunday excursions to the coast, this was usually the farthest south where one could regularly see 3/4-SUB electric units. Unit 4352; one of the new-build 1925 Eastern Section three-car formations, but now augmented to four cars, stands in platform three, having arrived with a service from London through Dorking North, circa mid-late 1950s. In platform four is a train of Maunsell vehicles; probably a steam-hauled connecting service to Steyning and Brighton, although onward electric services for all stations to Billingshurst, Pulborough and Littlehampton would be provided by 2-BIL electric units. Regular steam-hauled passenger services southwards ceased here when the branch to Guildford closed in June 1965 and when the line to Brighton through Steyning closed in March 1966; although this had almost a two-year period of diesel multiple unit provision before closure. Unit 4352 began life as a three-car unit 1522 in 1925 and was formed of motor brake thirds (now seconds) 8469/70 with composite trailer 9602 in the centre, running thus until August 1945. Bulleid ten-compartment trailer 10353 (the second coach visible) was then added, and the unit renumbered as 4-SUB 4352, running in this form until November 1961. *K. Coursey 115*

M7 0-4-4 tank No 30108 departs from Midhurst LBSCR station, passing the large attractive Brighton timber-clad signal box, and propelling an LSWR corridor pull-push set (one of 731-739) towards Elsted, Rogate and Petersfield on 11 February 1951. The LBSCR goods yard and goods shed are just visible behind the train. Despite the station being reasonably sited at the southern end of the town, the routes to Midhurst were always backwaters. The LBSCR arrived from the east through a tunnel; from Hardham Junction on the mid-Sussex line through Petworth (a station most definitely not well-sited for that town!) in 1866; by extending their line from Petworth that had previously opened in 1859. The LSWR had arrived at their terminus (sited to the west) two years earlier in 1864. A goods link was established between the two stations, also opened in 1866. The final line to arrive was another LBSCR venture, from Chichester and the south in July 1881, when the second (and enlarged) ex-LBSCR station was opened. However, what Midhurst really needed was a direct line northward towards London, but topography defeated that. The two companies' services continued to operate independently of each other until closure of the route south to Chichester for passenger traffic as an early casualty of road competition, in July 1935. Opportunity was then taken to revamp the service so through trains ran from Pulborough to Petersfield; thereby connecting the ex-LBSCR mid-Sussex line to the ex-LSWR Portsmouth direct, instead of having to change at Midhurst. However, traffic was clearly not there and even this sensible economy failed to stave off closure to all passenger traffic, which occurred on 5 February 1955: long before Beeching! This was one of few locations on the Southern where one could regularly encounter one-coach trains. Goods traffic continued from the Horsham direction only until October 1964. So light was the traffic that crews from there used to regard the week-long roster as a holiday! *R. C. Riley 4330*

Looking eastwards on 6 November 1954, we see the LBSCR passenger station with Q class 0-6-0 No 30545 having arrived with a goods train from Petersfield. In due course, it will reverse into the LBSCR goods yard before continuing its journey towards Petworth and Horsham. The two main platforms were originally used for up and down LBSCR services between Horsham and Chichester via Midhurst, while the bay now occupied by the goods train was used by the terminating LSWR service from Petersfield. Notice the two rusty lines in the right foreground. These led to the Chichester branch but use of these ceased abruptly on 19 November 1951. On that morning, a culvert south of Midhurst was washed out by heavy rain and C2X No 32522, hauling the daily goods train, plunged into the gap. Fortunately, the crew saw what was happening and were able to jump clear, but the loco was marooned in the bed of the stream for some months before recovery. That spelt the end of the route for through goods traffic, although the C2X was repaired and returned to traffic. *R. C. Riley 5626*

Top: We are now looking towards the LBSCR goods yard and station in the far distance with the former LSWR terminal station of 1864 on the left, again on 6 November 1954. The new (1866) alignment and the bridge over Bepton Road may be seen. The LSWR station was closed in 1925 and trains were diverted over the connecting line and into the LBSCR station from then on. Perhaps surprisingly, the LSWR station survives while there is no trace whatsoever of the former LBSCR station, which has disappeared under housing. The abutments of the Bepton Road bridge may still be seen, while to the east, the bricked-up mouth of Midhurst Tunnel is the only extant piece of LBSCR infrastructure. *R. C. Riley 5624*

Bottom: At Petersfield on 6 February 1955, LSWR T9's 30301 and 30732 are almost ready to depart with the next stage of the RCTS Hampshireman rail tour onwards to Havant, Fareham, up the Meon Valley to Alton, and to Frimley, where reversal took place enabling the train to reach Farnborough via Sturt Lane West Curve, where a further reversal allowed the train to return to Waterloo via the South Western main line. The board being held by the participant on the right was the RCTS headboard, which was affixed to the top lamp bracket before starting off. If on time, this will be about 1.20pm. The train was the last to run over the entire Meon Valley line, which closed the next day. The tour began at Waterloo and ran to Guildford via Staines and Chertsey behind LBSCR H2 Atlantic No 32421, then traversed the line through Slinfold to Horsham behind a pair of LBSCR radial tanks. It then reversed and reached Petersfield via Midhurst; one of several rail tours to reach Midhurst during the 1950s and early 1960s. *L. R. Freeman 1438*

A location unfamiliar to many railway enthusiasts; the LSWR terminus at Bishops Waltham on the branch from Botley. This was a visit by The Branch Line Society on 7 March 1959, and clearly a wet and windy occasion to judge from the clothing of those present! This was hauled by M7 No 30111, with hybrid LSWR/SECR pull-push set No 6. It started at Portsmouth Harbour at 12.33pm and ran to all the freight-only branches in the South Hampshire area, including Lavant, Bishops Waltham, Droxford, and Gosport, before returning to Portsmouth at 6.27pm. If on time, the train ought to have been at Bishops Waltham between 2.52 and 3.02pm. The Bishops Waltham branch was just four and a half miles long and opened in June 1863, closing to passengers on 31 December 1932. However, goods traffic continued until April 1962. At least three passenger specials visited the line in the 1950s and this was the final occasion. On 14 June 1952, one of them was hauled by C14 class 0-4-0 tank No 30589; sister engine to No 30588 seen at Southampton Docks in a later picture: a rare passenger duty for such a locomotive. *R. Hobbs 1336*

Spotlight on Eastleigh

The original station at Eastleigh; then named Bishopstoke after a small nearby village, open in 1841. It later became one of the most important locations on the South Western network. Renamed as Eastleigh and Bishopstoke in July 1889, it was the site of the carriage and wagon works from 1891 and the locomotive works from 1909 and one of the largest junctions on the system. It remains so today, but only part of the locomotive works remains in use, while the carriage and wagon works closed in 1968 and some of the staff transferred to the locomotive works, while others moved to Derby, York, etc. For many years it was, by an enormous margin, the largest employer in the town.

The station itself had four platforms and two through lines, several large goods yards, and a permanent way depot as well as the workshops, plus a large 15-road running shed to the south of the station. It was, and still is, the junction for the line south-eastwards to Fareham and Portsmouth, as well as the now single line westwards to Romsey and Salisbury. We will now look at the station, its surroundings, the locomotive works, and the extensive running shed: once home to more than 120 locomotives, never mind all those either leaving or awaiting attention in the nearby locomotive works. For the enthusiast, there was always plenty to see in and around Eastleigh.

Eastleigh's own T9 No 30120 at the down platform with a special to Portsmouth and Southsea on 11 October 1958. On leaving, the train will take a left turn beyond the platform, pass between the carriage works and the locomotive works on its journey towards Fareham and pass Eastleigh South signal box on the way. It has probably come from Reading. The stock is a mix of ancient and modern. The leading vehicle is a 58ft rebuilt LSWR third of 1890s vintage mounted on a 58ft SR standard underframe; one of several such rebuilds dating from between 1935 and 1936, followed by a pair of Bulleid three-coach sets type L and dating from between 1947 and 1948. The LSWR vehicle originally had eight compartments; it now has nine plus a pair of lavatories near the centre of the coach. The conversion involved splitting the original body in two and mounting them at each end of the new underframe: splicing an extra compartment and the lavatories into the resulting 10ft gap in the middle. Cut and shut or kit-bashing at 12 inches to the foot scale! Probably a method of reconstruction that, for safety reasons, would be frowned upon today. T9 No 30120 is now part of the National collection and is currently located on the Swanage Railway. Beyond the footbridge connecting the two island platforms, the extensive marshalling yard may just be glimpsed. This extended more than a mile up the line towards Allbrook signal box, while the carriage works buildings may be seen on the right. *R. C. Riley 12889A*

On 25 August 1957 at the up through platform, BR standard 2-6-2 tank No 82012 is attaching a GWR Python A van (No W580W; the one with a strengthened floor for carrying elephants!) to the rear of a train composed of BR standard set 889 hauled by a BR standard 2-6-0. No 82012 was completed at Swindon Works in July 1952, and went to Exmouth Junction shed, along with 12 others, but moved to Eastleigh in February 1953, and finally to Nine Elms in December 1962. So, 72A, then 71A, then 70A! It was withdrawn on 31 May 1964, the locomotive was still working locally three months later, but was cut up by Cohen's of Kettering in November 1964. BR standard set 889 was originally formed in 1952 of four coaches; two brake thirds, a corridor third and a corridor composite, but was augmented to six vehicles by the addition of another composite and an open third during 1954. The visible formation is therefore likely to be S34279, S24325, S15047, S15901, S3926, S34280 and the train is probably a Portsmouth-Salisbury-Bristol service; this being the regularly rostered duty for set 889 at that date. And as for carrying elephants: it's probably unlikely in this instance! *R. C. Riley 11121*

The next train on the down through on 25 August 1957 was Battle of Britain pacific 34090 *Sir Eustace Missenden Southern Railway* with the 10.14am Waterloo to Bournemouth West excursion; Nine Elms duty 43. The return working was at 7.56pm from Bournemouth West, giving passengers a good day out at the seaside. The engine still carries a 73A Stewart's Lane shed plate but was re-allocated to Nine Elms the previous June. Nobody has yet had time to change the plate, not exactly important in the scale of things! As rebuilt, the loco features again in a later photograph taken at Nine Elms in 1967. The 12-coach train is a mix of Maunsell and Bulleid stock; both in green and crimson lake and cream. On the left is Eastleigh West signal box, which controls the junction of the main line to Southampton and the Fareham/Gosport/Portsmouth lines, and the entry to the loco works and running shed. It contained 90 levers and was an LSWR type 3B box. Previously known as Bishopstoke West, it was renamed in 1899 and closed on 6 November 1966, when the new Eastleigh panel box took control over the whole layout. The photographer is standing between the up and down lines to Fareham. Eastleigh East box was at the other end of the station, and controlled the junction to Romsey, the marshalling yard, carriage works and carriage siding entries, plus the main line north towards Allbrook. *R. C. Riley 11122*

In complete contrast, the next down departure was a local service to Southampton Terminus; in fact, standing in the down platform as No 34090 passed: look back at the last picture! M7 No 30030 sets off with a LSWR 3-LAV set in tow, and will probably call at Swaythling, St Denys, and Northam before reaching its destination. It has probably come from Winchester City or Chesil station. The 3-LAV set comprises two Diagram 125 56ft brake thirds (now seconds) built between 1910 and 1911 with a rebuilt Diagram 285 58ft composite on Southern underframe in the centre; this rebuild dating from 1935. By now, just four such sets of this formation remained in traffic; this must be one of Nos 104, 109, 114 or 116. Note the slight differences in bodywork style between the vehicles. The M7 put in no less than 55 years' service; from February 1904 until October 1959; at Nine Elms, Feltham, Exmouth Junction and, finally, Eastleigh sheds. *R. C. Riley 11123*

A rather unusual visitor to Eastleigh is standing in the down loop platform. On 17 May 1953, ex-Plymouth, Devonport, and South Western Junction Railway 0-6-2 tank No 30757 *Earl of Mount Edgcumbe* waits to leave with an RCTS special to Fawley and Southampton Docks. Departure time was scheduled for 3.10pm and the 0-6-2 will take the train to Fawley, where USA tank No 30062 took over for the run back through Southampton Central. It then took a circular tour to both the old and new docks, before returning to Southampton Central at 7.10pm. There were two such PDSWJR 0-6-2's (plus a smaller 0-6-0 tank) built for the Colonel Stephens Callington branch in 1908, and both served there until 1957. Note the 72D Plymouth Friary shed plate. The pair would only make the long trek back to Eastleigh for routine overhauls, almost certainly the main reason for the loco being at Eastleigh in May 1953. The stock comprised three Maunsell open thirds (one from each of the 1933, 1935 and 1936 batches, with different window styles) and a BY passenger brake van. The Earl was one of the directors of the PDSWJR. His ancestral seat was once at Cotehele House, near Calstock (now National Trust), but for many years was at Mount Edgcumbe House. The current Earl's seat is now Empacombe House on the Rame Peninsular, also in East Cornwall. The family can trace their ancestry back at least as far as 1354. Of course, Great Western enthusiasts will think of a Castle class locomotive if the name is mentioned! The rather imposing ringed signal seen above the train is a LSWR lower quadrant provided by Stevens and Company, signalling engineers to the South Western. *R. C. Riley 4553*

Inside Eastleigh Works, we see H16 class 4-6-2 tank No 30517 stripped down and under overhaul; probably late Summer or early Autumn 1960; the last member of the class to receive workshop attention. For this reason, it was also the last in regular traffic; withdrawn in December 1962. The five members of this class were designed by Robert Urie and entered service between 1921 and 1922; working initially from Strawberry Hill shed on cross-London freight trains. Once Feltham shed and marshalling yard were operational, they were transferred there and remained so employed until 1959, when increasing use of diesels resulted in all five gradually migrating to Eastleigh for the Fawley oil trains. By late 1960, only No 30517 was found to be reliable, and the others drifted back to Feltham and storage. No 30517 eventually also returned late in 1961; then being employed on empty stock into Waterloo, van trains and goods trains to Nine Elms, Wimbledon, or Surbiton. However, the engine did participate in two suburban area rail tours during its final month in traffic in December 1962. They were powerful locomotives and BR afforded them power classification 5F; later uprated to 6F. In Southern days, they were used for Ascot race specials and could put in a good turn of speed when required. *R. Hobbs 1855*

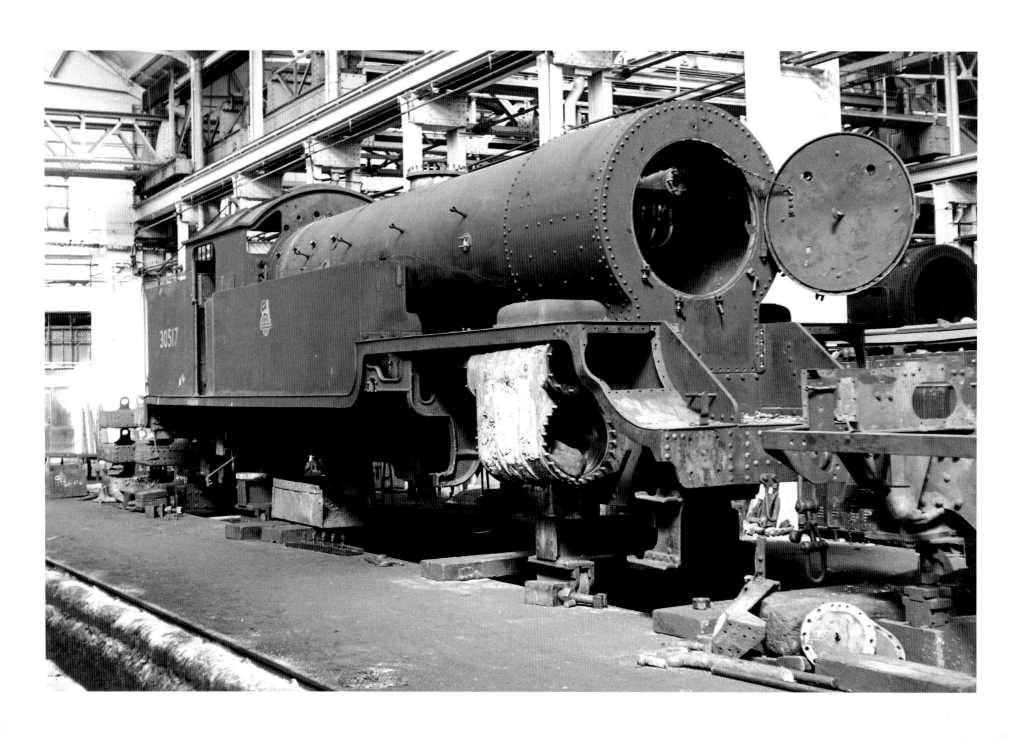

In a corner of the diesel workshop in September 1960, ex-LBSCR A1 class Terrier No 82 *Boxhill* is being prepared for transfer to Clapham Transport Museum. From 1920 until 1946, the engine was departmental shunter at Brighton Works, numbered 380s after June 1932 and never rebuilt to class A1X. For this reason, it was then restored to Stroudley condition and livery in time for an exhibition at Brighton Works in June 1947, another exhibition at Dorking North in September 1947, and the Waterloo centenary exhibition of 1948. The engine was then stored at Salisbury shed or in Farnham carriage sheds (along with LSWR T3 No 563; also in Eastleigh paint shop in September 1960) and made appearances at various other events during the 1950s, such as at Brighton in 1958, as seen in an earlier picture. By 1960, the finish had deteriorated and a further, albeit cosmetic, restoration was ordered. The engine moved to the National Railway Museum at York in 1976 where it remains today. *R. Hobbs 1860*

A later view inside Eastleigh Works, this time from October 1964. Pride of place goes to Merchant Navy 35004 *Cunard White Star* from Bournemouth shed. This loco would see the inside of the works just once more; in September 1965, before slipping violently at Hook on 28 October 1965, which caused broken and buckled coupling rods. Despite having received a light casual overhaul, further repairs were not authorised, and the loco was cut up by Messrs. Cohens on Eastleigh shed early in 1966. It joined 35020 in being the second Merchant Navy to be cut up here instead of being towed away for scrapping. Behind No 35004 is perhaps a surprise; BR Crosti-boilered 9F No 92028, from 2E Northampton shed. By this date, Eastleigh was overhauling steam engines from other regions and no less than 14 foreigners were present in the works in October 1964, and these outnumbered the Southern Region engines present. One or two of them are probably visible, but not identified. Straight ahead is BR standard tank 80084 from Redhill shed. Scheduled steam overhauls finally ceased here in October 1966 with pacific 34089. This event was recorded by the local press with chief erecting shop foreman Harry Frith doing a piece to camera for the local television news channel. A few engines did manage to creep in for minor attention before the end of steam in July 1967, but that was the last overhaul. *R. Hobbs 3417*

On 24 April 1953, No 35020 *Bibby Line* suffered a broken crank axle while travelling at speed near Crewkerne. Fortunately, the train was brought to a stand without derailment, but all members of the Merchant Navy class were then examined for similar defects. More axle flaws were found, and so from 12 May 1953 the entire class was taken out of service, pending fuller examination. No fewer than 19 other engines proved to have defects. The smaller pacifics were then subject to similar examination but only a few were found defective. The resulting motive power crisis was covered by the loan of other classes from the Western, Eastern and London Midland Regions, resulting in the sight of Britannia's, V2's, B1's and black fives on the Southern for a period of about three weeks. On 17 May 1953, No 35009 *Shaw Savill* from Salisbury shed stands at the side of Eastleigh Works minus the centre axle; one of those found to be defective. The engine was out of service from 13 to 22 May. Another classmate stands to the right. No 35009 was one of the second batch of MN's and these were characterised by the raised strengthening rib along the centre of the asbestos limpet board casing. Nos 35001/2 differed again, while the next ten (35011-20) had yet another incarnation of casing and the final ten (Nos 35021-30) yet another. Likewise, tenders also came in four patterns; increased still further after rebuilding and rebodying commenced. Modellers beware! *L. R. Freeman 834*

Sunday 17 May 1953, and clearly a society shed bash of some sort, where Dick Riley captured the prototype LN No 30850 *Lord Nelson* himself at the adjacent running shed: standing between two BR standard 4 moguls. These were Maunsell's largest locomotives; the first appearing in 1926, and for a short time the Southern Railway could lay claim to owning the most powerful express locomotives in the country, although this was soon eclipsed by the appearance of the GWR King class. However, in service the Lord Nelson's performance sometimes fell short of their potential power output, and several experiments and modifications took place to improve matters: few of which showed any improvement. When skilfully fired, few problems were encountered, but this was not always guaranteed. The arrival of Oliver Bulleid in 1937 meant a fresh appraisal of the class and, under his guidance, success was achieved, as well as an improved appearance to both locomotive and tender. By 1953, there were four members of the class allocated to Eastleigh but by 1956, this had risen to nine, increasing to all 16 by 1959. This ensured that crews became familiar with the class, and so got the best out of them. The usual duties included Waterloo-Bournemouth services, Southampton boat trains and inter-regionals as far north as Oxford. By this time, they were seldom seen on the West of England main line beyond Salisbury. No 30850 was withdrawn in August 1962 and placed in the care of the National Railway Museum. Restoration to working order took a long time but was completed at Carnforth in 1980 and the loco ran on the main line for several years; mainly in the north-west. Firebox problems caused the engine to be relegated to a static exhibit and it was not until 2009 that it started running again; this time at the Watercress Railway at Ropley. The boiler certificate expired in 2016 and the loco is currently awaiting overhaul. *R. C. Riley 4546*

At the rear of Eastleigh loco shed stands Battle of Britain pacific 34064 *Fighter Command*: clearly ex-works and probably just after the fitting of the Giesl oblong ejector chimney and blast pipe in April 1962. Dr Adolph Giesl-Gieslinger was an Austrian engineer who had studied steam locomotive technology and had developed his patent chimney in 1951. Increasing the draught on the fire reduced coal consumption by up to eight per cent along with a 20 per cent increase in power output. A considerable number of foreign locomotives were fitted this way, but BR restricted it to just two engines: the other being 9F 2-10-0 No 92250. Of course, they had to pay the designer a hefty licence fee, so perhaps this had some bearing on the matter! However, it was stated that reduction in fire-throwing was the main reason for the fitting; an undesirable attribute of the Bulleid pacifics in their original form. After some further modification to the equipment, crews found No 34064 to be much improved and some claimed that the loco was now equivalent in performance to the larger Merchant Navy class. Unfortunately, with the imminent demise of steam, no others were fitted, but in preservation, sister-engine 34092 *City of Wells* has been provided with one, and this has given good results. No 34064 only ran for four years in this form and was withdrawn in May 1966, having spent the last few weeks stored at Basingstoke shed. The sky-blue background to the nameplate shows up clearly; by this date West Country class engines had red backgrounds to their nameplates. Previously, under British Railways they had all been black. The locomotive's other claim to fame was as the thousandth engine to be built at Brighton Works; outshopped on 14 May 1947. *R. Hobbs 3374*

Eastleigh-allocated BR Standard 4 mogul No 76019 waits to leave Portsmouth and Southsea station with a through train formed of GWR stock heading for Bristol or Cardiff on 6 September 1955. By the position of the shadows, this looks like an early morning departure. It will probably come off at Salisbury, where a GWR loco will take over. The BR 2-6-0s came to Eastleigh from 1952 onwards as replacements for elderly ex-LSWR 4-4-0s. In fact, several South Eastern locos had been drafted to the area for a year or so before the advent of the BR engines; so, no doubt these were most welcome when they did arrive. Nos 76005-19 and 76025-29 were there by the end of 1953 but were joined later by others, bringing the SR total up to 42 of the class. No 76019 moved on to Bournemouth in August 1961 but was back at Eastleigh by September 1964 and was withdrawn from there in February 1966. Of the SR allocation, just No 76017 is preserved on the Mid-Hants Railway and based at Ropley, but there are three others that did not run on the Southern extant in preservation. *A. E. Bennett 884*

After Portsmouth, where better to go than across the Solent to the Isle of Wight? The Southern was unique in having a complete railway network that was physically isolated from the rest of the system and which presented the appearance of a working museum with elderly locomotives, carriages, and wagons; but nevertheless, ran efficiently. To an extent, the situation remains the same today, as the much-shrunk Island system still relies on cast-off rolling stock from the mainland. Three classes of locomotive worked there after 1933, although the last two LBSCR A1X tanks were returned to the mainland in 1949 in exchange for two more LSWR O2 tanks. Four LBSCR E1 0-6-0s were shipped over between 1932 and 1933, primarily to assist with coal trains but as this traffic fell away, they were more often used on passenger services. They were numbered one to four in the separate Island series. No 2 *Yarmouth* is seen on Newport shed, the usual allocation for Nos 1-3, on 26 June 1955, in company with No 1 *Medina*, visible behind. Built as LBSCR No 152 *Hungary* in October 1880, she lasted in Island service until September 1956. However, this loco is currently being recreated by the Isle of Wight Steam Railway at Haven Street, using 1877-vintage sister-engine No 110 *Burgundy* as the basis, so in time enthusiasts will once again be able to enjoy the sight of an E1 on the Isle of Wight. *Burgundy* was sold out of SR service as long ago as 1927, to the Cannock and Rugeley Colliery Company, where she worked in various guises until 1963. Then, after being sold into preservation, the engine changed hands several times, before being restored to working order at Cranmore, on the East Somerset Railway, running there from 1993 to 1997. Acquired by the Isle of Wight Steam Railway in 2012, the loco now requires extensive restoration, including a new boiler, before assuming the identity of *Yarmouth*. To date, a cosmetic restoration has taken place and the engine is currently on static display at Haven Street, finished in the livery seen here. *A. E. Bennett 235*

When the Southern took over the three Isle of Wight companies in 1923, there was an urgent need for modernisation of the system and almost immediately several ex-LSWR O2 0-4-4 tanks were shipped over. This process continued until 1949, by which time there were 23 examples of the class on the island, numbered between 14 and 36. No 31 *Chale* went over in May 1927 and was destined to be one of the final two working BR steam locos on the Island. She was retired in March 1967 having spent the final three months assisting with electrification works. No 24 *Calbourne* was used similarly and was soon purchased for preservation by the Isle of Wight Steam Railway. *Chale* was not so lucky and was cut up during late 1967. In better days, the loco is seen running round its train at Cowes on 26 June 1955, watched by enthusiasts and passengers alike. Once the loco has cleared the run round loop, the crossover will be reset and the coaches out of sight to the left will run down towards the buffer stops by gravity; the guard using the handbrake to control the train. No doubt a manoeuvre that would not be allowed today. Occasional buffer stop collisions were recorded, but none of a serious nature. The target 14 on the centre lamp iron refers to the IOW duty number. *A. E. Bennett 241*

A pair of impatient O2s wait at Smallbrook Junction for the road towards Brading on Saturday 4 July 1964. Perhaps an up train has been delayed over the single line, as this is the 7.50am van train from Ryde Pier Head to Shanklin and was usually double headed to get another O2 to Sandown for an early morning up train to Ryde Pier Head. The previous passenger train: the 7.40 from Pier Head, was also double headed to get an extra engine to Ventnor. Nos 20 *Shanklin* and 17 *Seaview* are anxious to get away from the signal check. This was typical on a Summer Saturday, when both single lines towards Ventnor and Newport-Cowes were at full capacity. Indeed, Smallbrook Junction signal box was a busy location tucked away in the countryside about a mile south of Ryde and smart work was needed to ensure that trains ran efficiently. It was also a fascinating place for the enthusiast to watch the action. The bogie brake van is one of four Island rebuilds of ex-SECR brake third coaches, Nos S1013-16, and the rebuilding dates from 1956, while the utility van is one of seven transferred to the Island in 1950, Nos. S1046-52, and, by a considerable margin: the newest items of passenger-rated rolling stock on the island. *A. E. Bennett 6472*

Back on the mainland at Southampton Docks during 1951, here is diminutive C14 class 0-4-0 shunter No 30588. Ten of these tanks were built under Dugald Drummond's watch between 1906 and 1909, primarily for use with pull-push trains of gated vestibuled stock. Completed as rather curious outside-cylindered 2-2-0 tanks with just the second axle powered, they proved useless in the role and, by 1911, most were out of use. Pull-push services were entrusted to larger locomotives instead. Drummond's successor, Robert Urie decided to rebuild five of the class as more conventional 0-4-0 dock tanks but only two were complete in 1913 before war broke out. The rest were offered for sale instead. Six found buyers, leaving just four in LSWR stock. One of the rebuilds was sold in 1917. The remaining two were similarly rebuilt as 0-4-0 tanks between 1922 and 1923: just three became SR stock. All were already on the duplicate list and were numbered 0741, 0744 and 0745. The latter was transferred to the Engineer's stock in October 1927 and became 77S at Redbridge sleeper works. The other pair eventually became SR Nos 3741 and 3744, finding employment mostly at Southampton Town Quay, where they remained until withdrawal in 1957. After Nationalisation they were renumbered as 30588/89 respectively. Staff referred to them either as Humpty-dumpties; presumably because they appeared as long as they were tall, or as Potato Cans; a rather less obvious derivation. The young fireman does not look like he is keen on being photographed. Maybe he is just as derisive of his engine! In fact, as dock shunters, they performed adequately. *L. R. Freeman H805*

Southampton Central on 26 June 1966. Rebuilt West Country No 34100 *Appledore* hauls the SCTS Devonshire Rambler special on its return to Waterloo. This departed from Waterloo at 9.55am behind original Bulleid 34002 *Salisbury* and ran, most appropriately to that city. From there, Merchant Navy 35023 *Holland Afrika-Line* took the train onwards to Exeter, then up the Western Region main line to Taunton and Westbury, where No 34100 took over. The return leg came via Salisbury, then through Romsey to Southampton, arriving there just before 5pm, as we can see! Unlike a good many enthusiasts' specials of the period, this one ran almost to schedule throughout and, although *Appledore* left Southampton a few minutes late, managed to record a two-minute early arrival at Waterloo. By now, electrification of the Bournemouth main line was in progress, note the conductor rails already in place, but replacement of the fine up-side buildings at Southampton Central had not yet started. Steam had its final complete Summer on the lines to Bournemouth and Weymouth. Even then, steam beyond Salisbury to Exeter was unusual and, as a result there were several specials billed as the last steam to Exeter. This was, most definitely, not the last one. The writer is amongst the throng on the platform but cannot be identified. *Dr I. C. Allen 69*

Bournemouth West station, 27 May 1958, looking towards the buffer stops on a quiet Tuesday lunchtime. This was the first station anywhere near the seaside and Bournemouth town centre. It opened quite late on; on 15 June 1874, the terminus of a branch line from Hamworthy and Poole. The original Southampton and Dorchester Railway main line (later absorbed by the LSWR) by-passed Bournemouth completely on its journey westwards, serving instead the established towns of Ringwood, Wimborne, Hamworthy and Wareham. It was known as Castleman's Corkscrew, after its main promoter Charles Castleman and the fact that it did not follow a very direct route. The direct line from Brockenhurst through Sway to Christchurch did not open until 1885, when the present Bournemouth station, which was previously Bournemouth Central, opened. Sometime later, Bournemouth West was served by a triangle off the main line and was a useful terminating point for services both from London and coming in from the west, either from Weymouth, Salisbury, or from the Somerset and Dorset Joint line. Closure came in October 1965, with all trains being diverted to Bournemouth Central, although a temporary closure a month earlier effectively spelt the end for most services. Today the station site is occupied by the A338 Wessex Way and a coach and car park. In this picture, we can see the station had six platforms, with two end-loading docks on the right which are hidden by the train of Bulleid stock in platform one. The small goods yard on the left dealt with coal and local goods traffic. A rake of ex-GWR stock stands in platform three, but the station seems remarkably quiet for what is presumably an ordinary weekday. Waterloo arrivals mostly used platforms five and six, departures usually occupied platform four, while local trains were dealt with at platforms one to three. Nowadays the buffer stops at the rear of Bournemouth train care depot are situated several hundred yards behind the photographer, alongside the A338. *L. R. Freeman 3368*

A stranger at Bournemouth Central on 30 May 1953. Ex-LNER V2 class 2-6-2 No 60893 departs for Southampton and Waterloo with the up Bournemouth Belle at 4.45pm. This was Nine Elms duty 35, normally diagrammed for a Merchant Navy pacific. As previously recounted, all 30 Merchant Navies were temporarily withdrawn from service following the failure of No 35020 *Bibby Line* near Crewkerne on 24 April with a broken crank axle. Similar and potentially serious crank axle flaws were found on about six of the class, with signs of defects in more than a dozen others. In the interim, the Southern borrowed several LNER V2's and B1's, some LMS Black 5's, several Britannia pacifics and BR class 5's to cover the shortfall, which lasted for about three weeks. This particular V2 was regularly entrusted with the Bournemouth Belle and performed most satisfactorily on the duty. Interestingly, when Bulleid was first formulating his plans for new Southern motive power, his initial ideas were for a 2-8-2 for the heaviest duties and a 2-6-2 for lesser services; mirroring Sir Nigel Gresley's plan of action using his P2 and V2 classes on the LNER. Of course, Bulleid was involved with the development of both designs. However, the SR Chief Civil Engineer, George Ellson; remembering the Sevenoaks derailment of 1927, vetoed both designs; which is how we came to have both the Merchant Navy pacific and the light pacific designs instead. One cannot help thinking that Bulleid may have been right about the 2-6-2, as this would have been a far better choice for the lighter trains west of Exeter. Maybe rather more economical, too! *R. C. Riley 4625*

A rather more typical loco at Bournemouth Central: Urie N15 class 4-6-0 No 30743 *Lyonesse* stands on the down through road on 26 July 1954. She carries the Bournemouth Central-Weymouth route head code, so is presumably going to take over the Weymouth portion of the next train in from Waterloo. Built in August 1919, she received the King Arthur character name in June 1925, running until October 1955 with a credited mileage of 1,301,442. BR Brunswick green livery is carried, which replaced SR malachite in June 1953; the last of the class to be repainted in BR colours. The highly distinctive smoke deflectors were fitted to this loco in November 1927 following wind tunnel tests carried out by London University with the aim of lifting the exhaust steam clear of the boiler and cab windows. Several different devices were tried but these proved the most effective and became a Maunsell locomotive trademark. They might have looked odd to start with, but time ensured that they blended in well on most Southern engines. Much SR publicity material of the thirties would feature them in the stylised outline of the engines. The Bournemouth shed plate, 71B, is clearly visible and Nos 30736-43 were so allocated at the time of this picture. They could regularly be found hauling expresses to Weymouth, Waterloo and through trains to the north as far as Oxford. *R. C. Riley 5166*

At the other end of the scale, at Bournemouth shed on 26 July 1954 we find LSWR G6 0-6-0 tank No 30260: a regular there from July 1948 until November 1958. The bunker handrail provides a handy place to store the fireman's shovel. The shed usually had one of the class on the books during the 1950s, occasionally two, and a regular duty would be to shunt Bournemouth Central goods depot, situated to the east of Holdenhurst Road bridge. This was on the site of the short-lived Bournemouth East station, which served as a rather inadequate terminus on the branch from Ringwood and Christchurch for just a few years before the direct line from Brockenhurst and the new Bournemouth Central station opened in 1885. The duty began around 3.40am each morning and continued right around to 2am the following morning, after which the loco returned to shed. Saturdays were different in that the duty ended earlier at 11pm. Four sets of enginemen were involved but it was probably not the most exciting of Bournemouth's duties. Clearly in company with a Bulleid, we do not know which one, but certainly not a Merchant Navy. Indeed, Bournemouth rarely had any of the bigger machines allocated; a few from new briefly for running-in between 1948 and 1949 and then not until after about 1957. Visitors from Nine Elms were, of course, common but by the time they were on shed, they would have been turned ready for a return to London. And just who E. Stevens might be we do not know either, apart from the fact that he has recorded his name in the dirt on the tender! *R. C. Riley 5167*

Activity at Wareham station on 9 July 1957. M7 class No 30105 has previously arrived in the up platform from Swanage hauling four coaches; the branch pull-push set and strengthening SECR coach S1093S, with the Bulleid brake composite in blood and custard on the rear of the train. Passengers will have disembarked from the branch set and the Bulleid coach will have been uncoupled in the platform. The M7 and PP stock will then have run round it via the crossover; blocking the level crossing while doing so, coupling to the other end, and then drawing the Bulleid coach out across a second crossover onto the down line behind the photographer to await the arrival of the N15 with the up train from Weymouth to Waterloo. This is formed of an LSWR Ironclad corridor third, now second, and a Maunsell three-set. No 30105 has now buffered the Bulleid coach onto the rear of the London train to provide the through service from Swanage. The shunters are now checking that the through coach is correctly attached to the main train and are about to uncouple the M7. All good entertainment for any enthusiast present. The M7 will now retire to the down bay on platform one, on the right to await the next down train while the N15 will depart once the level crossing gates have been closed. At Bournemouth Central another portion from Bournemouth West will be attached and the train, now probably between ten and twelve coaches in length, will proceed towards London. It was this sort of activity, and service provision, that made the steam railway so interesting. Yes, it could all be done today so much more simply using diesel or electric multiple units, but nothing like as interesting to watch! But of course, it just isn't done. *L. R. Freeman 2840*

Activity at the branch terminus. At Swanage on 14 September 1959, we see two more pull-push fitted M7s; No 30104 in the bay platform and No 30106 in the main platform. The former has just arrived, and the passengers are making their way towards the exit; perhaps after a day in Bournemouth as the shadows indicate late afternoon, while the latter has steam raised ready to depart. This was typical of the Summer Saturday service, with the single line branch being used to capacity. Trains could cross at Corfe Castle station and on the main line between Wareham and Worgret Junction, a mile or so west of Wareham station. There were also through coaches and complete through trains to and from Waterloo, plus a few other main line services from such locations as Basingstoke or Eastleigh. In the goods yard on the right are more coaches, possibly from a Waterloo train, while a departmental ex-LSWR van just creeps into shot on the right, standing behind the goods shed. Indeed, this may not actually be on rails; but standing on timber baulks or a short length of track isolated from the running lines and used to provide extra storage space. Fortunately, this scene may still be enjoyed today, as the present-day Swanage Railway has managed to reinstate the whole of the branch, including relaying most of the track after it was removed by BR in the 1970s, and has even managed a limited public service as far as Wareham. *H. Priestley PY10053S*

Another BR standard 4 2-6-0; this time No 76005 at Broadstone on a Bournemouth West to Salisbury service, date not recorded but probably 1963. Apart from a few mailbags on board the platform trolley, there does not appear to be much custom, even though the station had four platforms. Unfortunately, this was only too commonplace here as the Salisbury and Dorset line between West Moors and Alderbury Junction closed from 4 May 1964. It just failed to achieve a century of service, having opened in December 1866. The far platforms, Nos three and four, are on the original route of Castleman's Corkscrew towards Hamworthy Junction, but by this date, saw virtually no passenger trains at all. Platforms one and two served trains running from Brockenhurst through Ringwood and Wimborne towards Poole and Bournemouth West, until 4 May 1964. Trains off the Somerset and Dorset line continued to call until that line closed on 7 March 1966, leaving just local goods traffic to continue for a little while longer. Turn the clock back ten years and the motive power would probably have been a T9 4-4-0. *R. Hobbs 1515*

And another BR standard 4 mogul: No 76013 has left Bailey Gate station and passes Corfe Mullen signal box heading for the Corfe Mullen cut-off and Broadstone Junction; the tablet for the single line has just been collected. The train is the 6.48am from Bath Green Park to Bournemouth West, on 6 November 1964. We are now on the Somerset and Dorset Joint line proper and, although it looks like a double track leaving the crossing and heading eastwards, the left-hand line only leads to Carter's siding and the remains of the original S and D route towards Wimborne; closed as long ago as 1933. The train will take the crossover to the right-hand track and turn south across the golf course to Broadstone. By now, BR standards predominated on the Joint line, together with WR stock; a Hawksworth brake coach is visible. Closure was now just 16 months away and this was becoming increasingly apparent in the condition of the stations, engines, and stock; plus, the declining patronage as the Western Region, now in control of most of the line, sought to divert or dissuade whatever traffic remained elsewhere. Carter's siding, which served a clay pit, closed about 1959 but the line leading to it was used for condemned wagon storage, along with several other locations, until about 1965. *L. R. Freeman 8199*

The LCGB South Western Rail tour changes engines at Bailey Gate on 18 September 1960 at the southernmost S and DJR station. It is about to leave behind that most quintessential S and DJR locomotive; 7F 2-8-0 No 53804. The stock is most definitely from the Southern Region; BR Mk 1 Southampton boat set 352. This was a remarkable 12-hour trip from Cannon Street out around South London and then to Clapham Junction, Ascot, Alton, Eastleigh, Fawley and on to Broadstone, where the S&DJR loco took over for a run to Templecombe where the train reversed, then back to Salisbury, concluding with a sprint to Waterloo behind a T9. At least half a dozen locos were involved. Behind the station may be seen the United Dairies, later Cow and Gate, milk depot which produced both milk and cheese which went to London, and perhaps surprisingly, northwards to Templecombe, where it was integrated with the West of England milk trains from Devon. One would have thought that the journey would be quicker via Bournemouth, but no milk trains ran on those lines. The milk depot is no more, and the site is now occupied by a trading estate. Much has been written about the S and DJR, but by BR days it was perhaps an uneasy partnership between the Southern and the London Midland Regions, and running mostly through WR territory, too. In May 1948, the LMR proposed transferring the lot to the Southern Region: the locomotives and sheds, together with all eleven 7F 2-8-0s. This did not happen, although the Bath shed code did change to 71G, in the Eastleigh district, from 1950 to 1958. The LMR eventually reclaimed all their Black 5 4-6-0s, for use elsewhere on their system, to be replaced by BR standard classes instead, culminating in, from 1960, several Bath-allocated 9F 2-10-0s. Inevitably, the Western Region gained control in 1958 and this spelt the end for the joint line as through traffic was diverted onto alternative WR routes from September 1962. *A. E. Bennett 5302A*

Moving westwards to Yeovil Town; sometime in the Spring of 1964 as the shed plate on the Bulleid pacific is now 83D; the Western Region code for Exmouth Junction since October 1963. It had previously been coded 72A. No 34002 *Salisbury* was a long-term resident in the West Country, while U class mogul 31632 stands inside the shed and a GWR small prairie tank, either No 4591 or 4593; both Yeovil residents at the time, is alongside. By now the code for Yeovil was 83E, although the mogul carries no plate, and was formerly SR code 72C. There was a small GWR shed at Yeovil Pen Mill until 1959, but when this closed the remaining ex-WR engines and staff transferred to Town. Just visible inside the shed is a BR standard 3 2-6-2 tank from Taunton, indicating that the GWR line from there was still open, so the picture almost certainly pre-dated 15 June 1964. The shed opened in 1860; one of three similar shed buildings from this era, the others being at Salisbury and Queen Street, Exeter. This was the only one to survive until the end of steam, which at Yeovil occurred in June 1965. The other two were replaced by much larger edifices in the late 19th Century. Many local Salisbury-Exeter trains changed engines at Yeovil Junction; far more than seemed really warranted, and as a result Yeovil Town shed was quite busy with visiting engines from Exmouth Junction, Salisbury, and some of the depots further east. There had once been a small turntable here, but this was later removed, and a larger table installed at Yeovil Junction. Stabling of diesels continued here until 1968 and the yard was used as a collection point for recovered permanent way materials for at least one further year. The location is now a car park, cinema, and indoor bowling centre. *R. Hobbs 1798*

The next LSWR branch west was to Chard Town, which opened in 1863 but this did not last long as a South Western passenger service. The GWR broad gauge branch from Taunton arrived in the town in 1866 and the two lines were soon connected by a short spur, leaving the former LSWR terminus to serve as a goods depot. Separate LSWR and GWR trains continued to run into Chard GWR station until the First World War; long after the GWR line had been re-gauged in 1891. Since 1917, the Great Western took over the running of the whole line until passenger closure in 1962. The 1863 LSWR corrugated iron, or so-called tin, station building may be seen on the right, the platform now serving as coal staithes. The rather more substantial goods shed to the left also served until 1966, goods trains then arriving from Chard Junction station, three miles distant on the former LSWR main line to Exeter. Unlike most branches in the west, this one did not serve a holiday resort, so was by-passed both by through Waterloo trains and holiday passengers. *A. E. Bennett 4052*

On a rather quiet Sunday 5 May 1957, M7 No 30046 heads LSWR Ironclad PP set 381 at Seaton. The Seaton branch left the main line at Seaton Junction, traversing the picturesque Axe Valley to the terminus on the riverbank adjacent to the town and the sea. Unlike most West Country branches, this one was usually the preserve of pull-push operation. The station was largely rebuilt by the Southern Railway in 1936 and used many standard concrete components as well as a muribloc concrete single road engine shed, which replaced the original timber structure that was already in danger of falling into the river! The opening of a large Warner's holiday camp adjacent in 1935 had boosted traffic and through trains to and from Waterloo were a regular Summer Saturday feature until 1962. These reversed at Seaton Junction station, which itself had also been completely rebuilt by the Southern between 1927 and 1928. The holiday camp went through several changes of ownership since the 1980s and was demolished in 2008; the site is now occupied by a Tesco Supermarket. The Seaton branch closed in March 1966 and much of the track bed up to Colyton is now occupied by the Seaton Tramway, which itself is a fugitive from Eastbourne in 1970, while the station area is given over to a ramshackle collection of industrial units. *A. E. Bennett 2092*

A prosperous looking Topsham station, on the Exeter-Exmouth branch, seen on 25 May 1961. The original 1860 Sir William Tite red-brick station building has been painted over but remains smart; it wasn't always thus. The building, minus platform canopy, is now grade two listed but is no longer in railway use. British Railways Commer delivery van 3A1027S, registration No SLP 543, stands outside. One is not sure if it would be easier just to quote the registration number rather than the fleet number; however, the latter indicates three tons capacity and Southern Region allocation! Even the Southern Railway had an extensive fleet of road delivery vehicles and, by the 1950s, this had mushroomed under British Railways. The Exmouth branch remains open today, with a healthy commuter traffic and it was almost always so, in marked contrast to many lines on the Southern in the west. And do you remember those Holiday Runabout Tickets? They were available for specific areas but within those geographical boundaries you could travel by any train service. Great if you were spending a week at a holiday location at the centre of a well-connected rail network. You just had to keep within the published boundaries! *L. R. Freeman 5713*

On 25 May 1961, at around 3pm in the afternoon; original West Country pacific 34023 *Blackmore Vale* arrives up the one in 77 gradient into Okehampton with the Padstow and Bude portion of the Atlantic Coast Express. The coaches are a Maunsell 1936 open third (now second), two Bulleid Diagram 2406 loose brake composites and a two-set R from the series 63-75 on the rear. Most likely, the three at the front are for Padstow, with the rear pair for Bude, to be detached at Halwill Junction. The prominent loudspeaker was to ensure that station announcements were heard in the rear coaches of longer trains, invariably off the platform end, to ensure that passengers were in the correct part of the train for their destination as many Plymouth services would shed a North Cornwall portion here. The loco shed is on the left, with the 1947-vintage concrete coal stage visible. The muribloc shed itself is hidden by the locomotive. As is now well-known, the daily Exeter to Okehampton service was reinstated in November 2021, after many years of local campaigning. Whether the line onwards to Tavistock and Bere Alston reopens remains to be seen.
L. R. Freeman 5722

Opposite Top: One of the most rural lines in the west was the North Devon and Cornwall Junction Railway, from Halwill to Torrington. This only opened in 1925, and it was always far more important for goods than passenger traffic; mainly clay from Peters Marland. There were usually just two passenger or mixed trains each way each day; timed to suit the requirements of the clay works and their employees and comprising a single coach plus goods wagons as required. At other times, enthusiasts that ventured onto the line often found that they were the only passengers! This is Petrockstow, looking north (up) towards Torrington, on 1 June 1960, with the rear of a Bulleid Diagram 2406 brake composite coach visible. By now, the usual motive power would have been an Ivatt 2 tank from Barnstaple shed, but in earlier days, ex-LBSCR E1R class 0-6-2 tanks were employed. The station staff had time on their hands, so notice the immaculate platforms, complete with rhododendrons and the seven-lever ground frame controlling all points and signals. Levers one and two controlled the down home and starter, levers six and seven the up home and starter, while three and five controlled the points at each end of the passing loop, lever four the yard entry points. Not surprisingly, this was an early closure to passengers: on 1 March 1965, although an enthusiasts' special; the Exmoor Ranger, was the last passenger train over the line four weeks later. Clay traffic continued to pass northwards until September 1982. *L. R. Freeman 4760*

Bottom: The LSWR accessed Plymouth using the mixed-gauge GWR Launceston branch south from Lydford in 1874 but this was hardly a satisfactory arrangement. In due course, the Plymouth, Devonport and South Western Junction Railway built a well-engineered main line from Lydford through Tavistock, Bere Alston, the magnificent Tavy Viaduct and the Tamar Valley to access Plymouth by the back door. It opened in 1890. Part of it remains open today, serving Gunnislake via Bere Alston and still boasts a healthy commuter traffic to Plymouth. Not only did this line see the Plymouth boat expresses and trains from London through Exeter and Okehampton, but there were also local services from Friary up to Bere Alston, Callington and Tavistock. One of the latter, the 8.46am from Tavistock just to Bere Alston waits to depart on 27 May 1961 behind O2 No 30183, hauling one of the Maunsell 2-sets W numbered between 100 and 110, brake composite and open second, allocated to West of England local services. The train had arrived there at 8.33, as the 7.40 from Plymouth, and the loco has run round the stock and shunted to the down platform in preparation to return south. The train then spent much of the morning running between Bere Alston and Callington, before returning to Plymouth at 12.56pm. She made one more round trip to Callington in the early evening, before a final return to Plymouth just before 11pm. There were a number of these locals as far as Tavistock, and one that ran as far as Brentor or Lydford, throughout the day and for many years were monopolised by O2's, T1's and latterly M7's. A tender-first Bulleid pacific was also not unknown. One of the pair of ex-PDSWJR 0-6-2 tanks could also be seen on these services until 1957. *L. R. Freeman 5804*

Above: Returning now up the South Western main line. This is the through Plymouth-Brighton service leaving Yeovil Junction at 2.06pm on 10 July 1959 behind Battle of Britain No 34056 *Croydon*. The train is formed of a BR Mk 1 set in crimson lake and cream, but with a Maunsell buffet car in green cut into the formation, while another Bulleid brake coach in green can be seen as the sixth vehicle. There would have been a Portsmouth Harbour portion on the rear, detached at Fareham. Out of sight, behind the express the Yeovil Town gate pull-push set 373 and M7 will be in the up-loop platform. On the right, a rake of Maunsell stock stands in the up sidings, while a train of Bulleid vehicles waits in the down platform before proceeding westwards forming the 12.46pm Salisbury-Exeter Central stopper. In the down side bay, a BR standard 4 mogul awaits its next duty. On the far left, the old GWR Clifton Maybank goods depot appears moribund. Today, this area is occupied by the Yeovil Railway Centre, and this includes the former Southern Railway turntable, enabling the station to act as destination for several steam-hauled special trains. At other times, demonstration trains run up and down several hundred yards of re-laid sidings to the left of the photographer. Waterloo-Exeter St Davids trains still use the former up island platform but nowadays both these platforms are bi-directional. *R. C. Riley 13815*

Not one for Sunny South Sam; the character from the Southern's 1930s publicity material claiming that the sun always shines in the south! T9 No 30724 comes into Andover Junction on an unseasonal 29 August 1958 with a featherweight goods train from Basingstoke and is crossing over to the up yard. This comprises one LNER van, one LMS van and a Southern pillbox 25-ton brake van. On the right, Andover Junction A, previously East, signal box may be seen. B box, once suffixed West was at the western end of the station, on the up side. The advanced starting signals guard the junction of the main line to Basingstoke (straight ahead under the distant footbridge) and the line to Andover Town, Romsey, Eastleigh, and Southampton off to the right. This was closed as far as Kimbridge Junction on 7 September 1964. Beside the main Waterloo-Salisbury-Exeter route, the other line into Andover was the once independent Midland and South Western Junction Railway, whose route struck off northwards at Red Post Junction and traversed part of Salisbury Plain and the Wiltshire uplands towards Marlborough, Swindon, Cirencester, and Cheltenham. A useful cross-country link that unfortunately attracted little traffic, except in wartime, and closed to passengers on 9 September 1961, although certain parts remained open for goods traffic for some time afterwards. Indeed, traffic to the Army at Ludgershall remains today, still served from Andover. *A. E. Bennett 4144*

Along the MSWJR at Marlborough, Eastleigh-allocated U class mogul No 31618 waits with the 2.50pm Andover Junction to Swindon Town train on 19 September 1959, hauling a GWR two-coach B set. Departure may be imminent, as the loco is blowing off steam, but the crew appear in no hurry to rise from their seats on the platform. However, a southbound train is just arriving, so presumably they are waiting for the single line tablet before proceeding. This is formed of WR corridor stock, so probably a through service from Cheltenham to Southampton Terminus. The line became part of the GWR at Grouping; not what the independent company wanted, and their fears were probably realised as the line remained a backwater throughout the Grouping and BR eras. They were keen to join either the Southern or the LMS; as might be inferred from their independent title, but it was not to be. Once the stock of MSWJR locomotives were withdrawn, ex-GWR types predominated, but in the final few years, SR moguls started to appear; these were probably not to the liking of the Western Region crews either! All in all, the line was nobody's baby and closure became a foregone conclusion. *L. R. Freeman 4394*

A down West of England service passing Barton Mill sidings, east of Basingstoke behind Merchant Navy 35006 *Peninsula & Oriental SN Co* on 04 August 1964; just two weeks before being withdrawn from service. The loco was new in January 1942, going to Salisbury shed where she remained for her entire working life: a unique claim amongst the Bulleid pacifics. Rebuilt between August and October 1959, this was the last original MN on the South Western section. After withdrawal, the loco was stored at Eastleigh until March 1965, then being sold to Dai Woodham's scrapyard at Barry. Resident there for no less than 18 years, only the loco was purchased for restoration by the Gloucestershire and Warwickshire Railway, as the tender had already been sold to another group restoring a different Merchant Navy. This took a further 33 years, and included the construction of a new tender, enabling the loco to re-enter public service in May 2016. At the time of writing, the loco is operational and has visited several other heritage railways since 2016. The train is just eight coaches, so relatively light, but 4 August was the Tuesday following the August Bank Holiday, so perhaps that explains things. The stock comprises BR Mk 1 three-set 529, with the composite replaced by a Bulleid vehicle, a BR Mk 1 brake composite, BR buffet and dining car with a Bulleid two-set on the rear and may be the 1pm from Waterloo to Exeter and beyond. Through working from Waterloo beyond Exeter St Davids would cease just a month later as Western Region control of all former Southern lines west of Salisbury finally took full effect. Life would never be the same again… *A. Swain Q21-4*

Running in after rebuilding at Eastleigh, the first light pacific rebuild, No 34005 *Barnstaple* is setting the stock of the 5.16pm from Portsmouth and Southsea back into the up sidings at Basingstoke on 9 July 1957. The first Merchant Navy rebuild, No. 35018 appeared in February 1956. From June 1957, it was the turn of the West Country and Battle of Britain classes. However, while all 30 of the larger engines were dealt with, a halt to the programme was called after 60 of the 110 smaller engines had been done, leaving 50 examples to run their mileage in the original condition. This was partly because some West of England lines could not be cleared for the rebuilds because they were heavier, but also due to the end of steam traction coming sooner than had originally been envisaged. No 34005 was a Nine Elms engine, note 70A shed plate and was expected to return there but a decision was soon taken that the rebuilds should first be concentrated on the South Eastern section. There were more opportunities there to make better use of their capabilities and it was a little while before they became common place on SW section services. From 1957 until 1961 Stewart's Lane and then Bricklayers Arms sheds became the allocation. Apart from the Exeter-Okehampton-Plymouth line from late 1960, the rebuilds remained barred from West of England routes. No 34005 returned to the South Western section in February 1961 and was withdrawn from Bournemouth shed in October 1966. It had previously been withdrawn in November 1965 and reinstated for the extra Christmas traffic, which clearly lasted for some time! *L. R. Freeman 2857*

At Basingstoke shed on 23 August 1957 is Urie King Arthur No 30748 *Vivien*, standing alongside the coaler; a typical steel and corrugated asbestos structure. The 20 Urie Arthurs date from between 1918 and 1923 as LSWR class N15 and were the basis for Maunsell's later improved versions. Not that they carried names, until the new Southern's Public Relations Office, John Elliot, hit on the brilliant idea of naming the new express engines after Knights and other characters and places from the legend of King Arthur. This, of course, supposedly gave rise to Maunsell's typically Irish humour suggesting that naming them would not make them run any faster. Apocryphal? Perhaps, but it makes a good story. Both Urie and Maunsell made several improvements to the original 20 engines. They were perhaps not quite as free running as the pure Maunsell versions but nevertheless all put in sterling service on South Western section routes until the mid-1950s. No 30748 was within a month of withdrawal when photographed, but that is certainly not apparent from the appearance seen here. Previously a Nine Elms engine, reallocation to Basingstoke took place earlier in 1957. A small detail of note; there are electric lights below each lamp iron position: a relic of the abortive Government-sponsored conversion to oil burning of 1947-1948. *N. Nicholson 1383*

Top: A Reading-bound train is about to leave platform eight at Guildford, behind T9 4-4-0 No 30732. The crew are clearly ready to go, and the fireman is looking back for the tip from the guard, but there is evidently a delay. The stock is a Maunsell restriction 0 Hastings line three-coach formation; the first digit of the set number, 9, is just visible so this will be in the range 940-950. The date is recorded as May 1959 when the loco was, surprisingly for a Redhill to Reading duty, still allocated to Fratton. Reallocation to Eastleigh took place soon after and withdrawal came in the following October. Maybe the loco was in transit between the two sheds? On the left, in platforms six and seven (there is one line between the two platforms), a 2-BIL electric may be glimpsed on a Portsmouth-Waterloo stopping service, while part of the yard and the loco coaling plant may be seen on the right. The long, green-painted footbridge spanning the entire layout appears overhead. *R. Hobbs 1353*

Bottom: Guildford shed was located between the Farnham Road overbridge and the mouth of Guildford tunnel, in a somewhat restricted site. Much of the layout was a roundhouse accessible only via the 55ft turntable, so a small pilot locomotive was regularly employed to shunt engines into and out of the shed roads. There seemed to be something of a tradition of using former Southampton Dock shunters, short wheelbase tanks. Over the years saddle tanks *Clausentum* and *Ironside* were used but by the mid-1950s it was the turn of the B4 0-4-0 tanks. Latterly, a USA 0-6-0 tank was allocated until the end of steam in July 1967. On 19 March 1961, B4 No 30089 was in use and was the regular engine from 1959 to 1963. By this time, there were just three of the class remaining, out of a total of 25 built. The other two could be found at Winchester City and Poole Quay. For their size, they were remarkably powerful and, in their days working within Southampton Docks, they could be called upon to shift considerable loads. *R. Hobbs 2043*

Possibly the most well-photographed duty for a Southern engine ever: Battle of Britain No 34051 *Winston Churchill* hauls the great man's funeral train through Mortlake on 30 January 1965, en route to Handborough, Oxfordshire, watched by crowds from the lineside. The writer was one stop up the line; at Barnes to see the train pass on that bitterly cold January day. He arrived there just in time to see No 34064 *Fighter Command* come through about an hour earlier to stand as the spare engine at Staines. The head code was specially agreed beforehand; in the form of a V to remember Sir Winston's familiar Victory salute. The train was formed of five Pullman cars and gangwayed bogie utility van S2464S, which acted as hearse van. It had been specially repainted in umber and cream livery to match the Pullmans as far back as July 1962 and then stored under cover at Stewart's Lane depot in the meantime. Not surprisingly, both the locomotive and the hearse van, plus at least one of the Pullman cars have since passed into preservation. This was the last occasion when a steam locomotive participated in a state funeral event. *L. R. Freeman 8218*

No prizes for guessing where: despite the presence of a Great Western pannier tank. M7 No 30321 keeps company with 57XX No 9770 at Clapham Yard on 13 August 1960. By this date, the M7s were gradually being displaced from Waterloo empty stock workings and several GWR pannier tanks were drafted in as replacements. Some were formerly used at Folkestone Junction, but this example only saw brief trials there in 1958, before coming to Nine Elms. They did not last long. By 1963, most ECS was in the hands of BR standard tanks. Nine Elms crews did not rate the ex-GWR locomotives very highly; maybe not surprisingly, even though they were more powerful and certainly younger that the locomotives that they replaced. The coach just visible to the left is interesting; S7715S, one of just two Maunsell brake firsts that had been rebuilt from pantry brake firsts in 1949 and regularly used on Southampton boat trains. Notice also that all the carriage sidings are numbered; there were almost 50 of them. *R. Hobbs 1774*

A few minutes past 11am and the down Atlantic Coast Express approaches Clapham Junction behind Merchant Navy 35020 *Bibby Line* on Monday 25 September 1961. The loco clearly has a good head of steam but has slowed to observe the 40mph speed restriction through the sharply curved South Western main line fast platforms. Ironically, they have the slowest line speed of all the 17 platforms through the station; well, perhaps bar those off the West London line, but these would seldom see expresses passing. The ACE was the fastest train to the west from Waterloo; averaging 60mph over the entire line to Exeter Central, stopping at just Salisbury and Sidmouth Junction. It was easily the quickest train to Exeter and even beating those on the Western from Paddington. But it was not to last and with Western Region take-over of the route beyond Salisbury in January 1963, all was set for a reduction to secondary main line status, which became effective from September 1964. The ACE made its last run on 5 September 1964, after which only an almost all-stations basic two-hourly service was provided west of Salisbury, with no advertised through connections beyond Exeter St. Davids. No 35020 was destined to enter Eastleigh Works for a final minor overhaul in February 1965, but clearly more major defects were found once the engine was stripped down and withdrawal was ordered instead. The writer visited the works on a school society guided tour at half-term, only to find the grim chalked message on the front framing: 35020 for scrap. She was one of only two Merchant Navies to be cut up there. 35004 was dismantled on Eastleigh shed by Messrs Cohen's about a year later, all other disposals were to either Sheffield; Nos 35002 and 35015: the rest to South Wales scrap merchants. Apart, that is, from the eleven preserved examples of the class; most of which came from scrapyards anyway. *L. R. Freeman 6648*

8 July 1962 and No 35020 again, seen outside Waterloo and about to reverse onto its train in the terminus; the shunt signal is off. We have no idea what the train is, as no route discs or duty numbers are displayed; just the tail lamp for working light up from Loco Junction at Nine Elms. Also standing at the up-home signals is M7 No 30032; on carriage piloting duties and carrying Nine Elms duty number 146. The 1936 Waterloo signal box may be glimpsed behind and contained three lever frames; one of 75 levers, one of 159 levers and one more of 75 levers; serving the main local, main through and Windsor lines respectively. It also controlled all points and colour light signals out to Vauxhall. This was manned by four signalmen and two booking boys, and it replaced at least three mechanical boxes that had previously controlled the track layout. The box continued in use, albeit with some changes to control arrangements in 1984, until 30 September 1990. It was then demolished to accommodate the Waterloo Eurostar terminal platforms, which are now in themselves history, since Eurostar moved to St Pancras International in November 2007. After a period of disuse, they are now used in modified form to serve the current South Western train franchise. *A. Swain M21-6*

A view in the opposite direction, taken from the end of platforms seven and eight; usually occupied by Portsmouth electric services. The signal box may be seen above the trains, while Salisbury's N15 No 30448 *Sir Tristram* shunts across the station approach. Perhaps it will eventually back down onto the plywood-bodied utility van visible at the end of platform ten, where the shunter is waiting to couple up. Platforms nine and ten were the usual choice for West of England trains. The motive power inspector is heading for the boarded crossing to reach his cabin located at the end of platform 11 and hidden by a set of BR Mk 1 stock. The occupants of this office would periodically clear the assembled throng of enthusiasts who gathered at this vantage point; especially if they became unruly, so good behaviour was essential to trainspotting at this location! The writer was only requested to leave once, because of a special train arriving from Portsmouth with a contingent of navy personnel on board; there must have been security implications. No 30448 was one of ten King Arthurs nominally rebuilt from Drummond 4-6-0s, but little of the original engines remained; perhaps confined to the cabs, smoke box doors and the tenders. However, the tender seen here is not the original; as the water cart originally paired with No 30448 was replaced by a more modern Urie pattern tender from H15 No 30478 in May 1955. The locomotive was withdrawn in August 1960, credited with having travelled 1,483,140 miles during its 35-year lifespan. *A. E. Bennett 3785*

Top: M7 No 30032 again; still carrying duty number 146 and waiting to leave platform nine at Waterloo with empty stock for Clapham yard on Saturday 1 July 1961. Alongside, in platform eight is N15 No 30451 *Sir Lamorak* on a train for Salisbury. This is possibly the 8.54pm departure, as the station lights are on, and the locomotive carries lamps, rather than discs showing that the journey will end after darkness has fallen. This will be fast to Woking, then all stations to Salisbury. By this time only Nos 30451 and 30453 *King Arthur* himself remained of the 448-457 series of nominal rebuilds. The class namesake was withdrawn before the month was out, leaving *Sir Lamorak* as the sole representative of the batch for a further 12 months and allocated to Salisbury throughout.
A. E. Bennett 5699

Bottom: A view across the buffer stops at Waterloo on 13 August 1960. At platform 13 is M7 0-4-4 tank No 30132 with empty stock from Clapham Yard, while at platform 12 is S15 4-6-0 No 30840, having probably arrived with a local service from Basingstoke or Salisbury. This was a Feltham-allocated loco and the class was much-used on Summer Saturday relief trains. Despite being nominally heavy goods engines, they invariably gave a good account of themselves. Across the wider expanse of the cab road, ex-GWR pannier tank 4681 may be seen in platform 11, having hauled the empty stock of a Southampton boat train, BR MK 1 set 353, up from Clapham Yard. The Ransomes and Rapier hydraulic buffers may be seen and are a feature of all the older platforms at Waterloo. They were the unlikely subject of a 1938 W. D. & H. O. Wills cigarette card in a series on railway installations. This depicts the buffer guides, out of sight to the left in red, but in more recent times they have been repainted blue. The sparkling white loco lamp is also worthy of note, as is the Tilly lamp alongside. *R. Hobbs 1771*

Schools class 4-4-0 No 30904 *Lancing* departs from Waterloo with a local train to Basingstoke on Saturday 13 May 1961, watched by a couple who have found a good use for a luggage trolley. The station lights are again illuminated, and a headlamp is carried on the engine, while the clocks read 7.54pm. The train formation is a Maunsell corridor second, followed by a Bulleid three-set and a utility van on the rear; the latter detached at Woking. By now, the Hastings line had no need of the class, so they were being used on such services as this, the Oxted line, the Reading-Guildford-Redhill line, and other less exacting duties. *Lancing* only had a few more weeks' service remaining and was taken out of traffic in July 1961. She was one of about half a dozen of the class to be allocated to Basingstoke shed, coded 70D, between 1960 and 1962. Nearly every member of the 40-strong class achieved over one million miles in service, and they could justifiably claim to be Maunsell's greatest design. Three examples escaped the breakers and may be found on the Watercress line, the Bluebell Railway, and the North Yorkshire Moors Railway. *A. E. Bennett 5485*

A stranger at Waterloo; certainly in 1961 but perhaps not half a century earlier. Adams radial tank No 30582 was brought up from the Lyme Regis branch to power two enthusiasts' specials around the SW suburban lines in March and April 1961. Organised by the Railway Enthusiasts Club; REC as seen on the LSWR-style diamond-shaped head code disc; this was the first tour on Sunday 19 March. The route was from Waterloo platform 16 departing at 1.58pm; out to Windsor and Eton Riverside, then to Guildford via Staines West Curve and Woking, then to Leatherhead LSWR station and back to Waterloo platform one, scheduled to arrive at 6.32pm. Rolling stock was hybrid LSWR/SECR pull-push set 1 plus a loose strengthening SECR 100-seat third; now second. These may be seen in the background. The tour appears to have been re-run on 13 April, but this does not seem to have been recorded on the Six Bells Junction website. Platforms 16-21 at Waterloo served the Windsor lines and were then the oldest part of the structure, dating from between 1884 and 1885. They were incorporated into the 1905 to 1922 complete rebuild of the station but were swept away in 1990, prior to construction of the Eurostar terminal platforms. Adams radial No 30582 was one of a class of 71 4-4-2 tank locomotives built between 1882 and 1885 for London area suburban work. Increased traffic soon saw them rusticated to the countryside and all except two were withdrawn by 1929. The last pair remained gainfully employed on the Axminster-Lyme Regis branch where, joined by another class member sold off in 1917 and re-purchased by the Southern Railway in 1946, the trio continued to serve until 1961. No 30583, the re-purchased example, may now be seen on the Bluebell Railway but is currently out of service, although intact and painted just as No 30582 seen here. *A. E. Bennett 5352*

Top: Perhaps a lucky shot, taken from a 4-SUB unit on the up Windsor local line between Queens Road Battersea and Vauxhall, this shows T9 No 30718 leaving Nine Elms goods yard on 1 June 1957. The destination is unknown, as the head code shown is not listed for the area but it's probably local. Nine Elms duty 48 included a van train around the Kingston loop in the small hours as well as a trip to Reading with more vans and some empty carriage stock workings into and out of Waterloo. By this time, T9s were a rare sight in the London area and No 30718 was one of the last three of the class shedded at Nine Elms; the others were 30338 and 30719. All moved away to Exmouth Junction in June 1959, to end their days on the North Cornwall line two years later. We will now move across the main line to the south side and end our circuit of the Southern Region at Nine Elms shed. *L. R. Freeman 2800*

Bottom: Nine Elms on 12 May 1965: still a fully working depot with plenty going on. Rebuilt Merchant Navy 35029 *Ellerman Lines* stands in the late afternoon sunshine, in the now roofless area of the old shed surrounded by other Bulleid pacifics. She still looks impressive. The penultimate member of the class, dating from February 1949, she was new to Bournemouth shed. Named by the chairman of the shipping company, Mr. A. F. Hull at Southampton Docks on 1 March 1951, the engine was allocated to Dover and could be seen on the Night Ferry and other boat trains into Victoria, until she returned to the South Western section and Nine Elms in June 1955. Rebuilt at Eastleigh between June and September 1959, the loco remained a Nine Elms resident until transferred to Weymouth shed in September 1964: along with several other Bulleids. This was perhaps a paper transfer rather than reality; Weymouth still had a full complement of fitters, whereas at Nine Elms recruitment was becoming difficult. The locos were still rostered for the same duties, just from the opposite end of the line. After withdrawal in September 1966, the loco remained at Weymouth until April 1967 before removal to Dai Woodham's scrapyard at Barry Docks; one of about 250 engines seen by the writer a few months later. In 1974 the loco was rescued by the National Railway Museum and is now displayed as a sectional exhibit at York, illustrating the inner workings of a steam locomotive. A very popular exhibit. *A. Swain S10-5*

Nadir at Nine Elms

For our final group of pictures, we remain at 70A Nine Elms shed. This was once the South Western section's premier locomotive depot, with an allocation of up to 126 engines. No dates are given by the photographer Paul Hocquard, but clearly, we are well into 1967. The end is nigh; finally taking place on 9 July with the cessation of all BR steam operations in the south of England. We all thought there might be some sort of renaissance or afterlife, but there was none, and BR issued firm instructions stating that no Southern steam locomotives were to be used under any circumstances. The notices even listed the locomotive numbers in case of any doubt. By the end, the throng of enthusiasts present could easily outnumber the staff. Similarly, the numbers of withdrawn or stored engines could easily exceed those still serviceable. While enthusiasts revelled in all this, it was painfully evident that many of the staff did not. They had to contend with outdated and dilapidated equipment, dirt and what was often heavy manual labour in cold, primitive, and badly lit buildings. Much of the infrastructure still bore the scars inflicted during World War Two, such had been the lack of investment during the post-war era and Nine Elms had had its share, with much of the old shed roofless and open to the elements.

Below: After closure, the shed lingered for a while. The last locomotives were towed away to the breakers by April 1968. Demolition then followed and by 1971 Sir Robert McAlpine and Co had taken possession of the near empty site. Construction of the New Covent Garden Market began and was complete in 1974. The writer worked there as a site engineer during this period, but by then almost all trace of the former railway infrastructure had been removed and it was difficult to imagine how it had once been. The old shed entrance from Brooklands Passage can still be seen, if one knows where to look, but beyond that; nothing now remains. One more picture from 1967 may be found on the rear cover.

The view from the pedestrian entrance at Brooklands Passage and one full of anticipation for enthusiasts about to bunk the shed. However, by 1967 things would be entirely predictable with the selection limited to just Bulleid pacifics, the odd Ivatt 2 tank and five classes of BR Standards. Of course, in earlier years it would be very different. The general air of dilapidation is evident; with an ash grab crane in the foreground, weeds, and piles of clinker everywhere, the coaler and shed buildings looking uncared-for. Few locomotives are visible. The turntable is away and out of sight in the corner to the far left. The chimneys of Battersea Power Station loom above the shed roof, and are lazily disgorging white smoke into the blue sky. According to some of the contractor's staff who were engaged on site clearance work, much of the infrastructure seen here took a great deal of demolition! *P. Hocquard 1274*

Left: Rebuilt West Country 34036; *Westward Ho* is seen across the loco yard, from the corner of the main building. It will soon run forward and turn on the turntable. The engine is blowing off furiously at 250lbs per square inch. Two members of staff are up on the tender trimming coal, and the photographer has managed to capture a feral pigeon silhouetted in the steam! There were always plenty of them about, although not so many white ones. Dilapidation is all around, with ineffective lighting as well as an end-on view of a water column. There were no less than 14 of them around the depot. *P. Hocquard 3764*

Right: Ash clearance was a perpetual job, and this poor chap could be at the task for the rest of his life! There were mechanical grabs to assist in the process, but they could not reach everywhere; good old manual labour was the last resort. No wonder recruitment was almost impossible by the mid-1960s, and one of the best reasons to finish with steam. By that date, nobody wanted to work under these conditions. *P. Hocquard 3398*

Two locomotives that were still going at the end. This is Merchant Navy 35003 and Battle of Britain 34090: both now shorn of their magnificent nameplates; *Royal Mail* and *Sir Eustace Missenden, Southern Railway*. They stand in the roofless area of the old shed, approximately where we saw 35029 in an earlier photograph. Notice that 35003 displays a red not to be moved sign as the left-hand side motion has been dismantled for some re-metalling of the bushes to take place; perhaps because of doing the ton a few days previously. Movement would upset the valve timing and make things very difficult for reassembly with the manual labour and hand jacks available. Yet, the engine is in steam, so, presumably whatever defect needed urgent attention. Or maybe, there simply wasn't an alternative loco available. No 35003 was by then the oldest Bulleid in traffic; running from September 1941 until July 1967: rebuilt between June and August 1959. The rebuilding included a complete reconstruction of the tender tank; identifiable by the fact that only a single ladder is now carried. The opportunity to increase the water capacity from 5000 to a nominal 5250 gallons was also taken, but in fact the capacity was found to exceed 5300 gallons. Tender reconstructions took place at Ashford Works, even though the locomotive rebuilding took place at Eastleigh. Her final duties appear to have been the 8.35am Waterloo-Weymouth and 5.49pm back to Bournemouth on 7 July 1967. The loco returned light to Weymouth shed, before being towed away for scrapping at Cashmore's in Newport, which took place in December. No 34090 was the last of the batch of twenty light pacifics ordered in early 1948 and appeared from Brighton Works on 1 February 1949. The engine received a special paint finish; uniquely carrying both malachite green with the three go faster yellow stripes, but also the BR Cycling Lion emblem. It was named officially by Sir Eustace at Waterloo on 15 February 1949, before taking up duties at Ramsgate shed. Rebuilt between June and August 1960, the loco was then allocated to the SW section and the final duty may have been in the Southampton area hauling the weed killing train on 11 June. By August 1967, the loco was with 54 others awaiting disposal from Salisbury shed and was cut up by Cashmore's in March 1968.
P. Hocquard 1261

Three men and a trolley! What may be the cause of 35003's problem; a hefty connecting rod is manhandled across the tracks into the workshop area. Here it will be turned through 90 degrees and wheeled down to the benches at the far end for re-metalling of the bushes. And then it must come back again and be lifted into position between the crosshead and the four locating studs on the centre driving wheel, with possibly just a couple of jacks for assistance. Other Bulleids lurk nearby including an original in the far shadows. By January 1967, just seven of these remained and by June just Nos 34023/102 were still serviceable. This is possibly one of Nos 34002/15/19/57; all withdrawn in the early months of 1967 and still at Nine Elms in July. The whereabouts of the missing one; No 34006, at this date is not known but maybe had already been dispatched to Cashmore's at Newport. *P. Hocquard 3729*

Left: Contrast in light, darkness, and front ends. An original Bulleid and a rebuild, the latter seen through an opening between the new shed and the roofless area of the old shed. The solitary tungsten filament light bulb provides little useful illumination! Neither locomotive can be identified.   *P. Hocquard 3752*

Right: Attention is given to the brake cylinders on the rear of 34090's tender. Wellies seem like a good idea! The inspection pit is full of clinker and water, so either clearance has failed to take place, or the drainage is blocked: probably typical and guaranteed to make a thankless task even more thankless. *P. Hocquard 1260*

Next up a hydraulic test on the boiler: fill it with water from one of the hydrants in the six-foot, put it under pressure and see what leaks. By this date, that's very likely and caulking will be the next task. At least these members of staff are looking mildly cheerful, but whether the representative of the Windrush Generation found Nine Elms to be his perfect idea of Great Britain seems doubtful. It was hard, heavy, and dirty work; none too well paid, either! Hopefully, the camaraderie made up for this just a little.
P. Hocquard 3721

A conversation alongside the weighbridge; was it work being discussed, or maybe the prospect of redundancy? This piece of equipment, manufactured by Messrs. Pooley and Son, was an essential item in ensuring that locomotive weight distribution was correct, and that springs were appropriately adjusted. The four plates in the track had their counterbalance arms mounted in the columns alongside, and the whole was protected from the elements by a somewhat makeshift timber and corrugated iron cover. This machinery was in the bombed-out part of the old shed; it had originally been under cover. The inset picture shows the name cast into the framing; H. Pooley held the contract for maintenance of most of the Southern Railway's weighing machines; there were lots of them; both big and small, and there was a fleet of mobile workshop vans in the departmental stock list dedicated to this task. These would travel the system on a regular basis together with their staff to check that the machinery was working correctly. The chair on the right has certainly seen better days and the hefty padlock looks like overkill considering the state of the timber doors! Unfortunately, by this time tools and equipment were not being replaced and had a habit of disappearing. Some staff took to carrying theirs home with them: items as shovels, fire irons, buckets, and the like. *P. Hocquard 1254 and 1255*

A member of staff deep in thought; oblivious to No 34087 shrouded in steam and setting off behind him. Note the state of the building structure; encrusted in soot from countless chimneys. Those little slatted metal trolleys were used to carry equipment around the site. The place was vast, so they came in useful.
 P. Hocquard 3767

Battle of Britain 34087; once *145 Squadron* reverses off shed towards the turntable with cylinder drain cocks fully open. This ensured all condensed water was cleared from the cylinders as soon as possible to prevent damage. The skeletal remains of the shed building are seen overhead; no doubt the residents of those flats probably welcomed 9 July 1967, and some peace and quiet. They alone are still there; shielded by trees from the comings and goings of New Covent Garden fruit and vegetable market Today it's a 24-hour operation, just as Nine Elms shed was.
P. Hocquard 3775

Off duty and homeward bound, two members of staff pass 80133 on shed road nine at the end of their shift. The flats in the surrounding streets may be their destination. The single-storied light-coloured buildings glimpsed in the haze in front of the flats are the administration offices and canteen. The exit to Brooklands Road is also just to the left of the ash grab crane. And with them, we say goodbye to our tour of the Southern Region. I trust you have enjoyed the journey.
P. Hocquard 3758